Revise
KS3
History

Christopher Lane

Contents

History at Key Stage 3

Introduction to KS3 History

This book is designed for you to use at home to support your study at school. The topics covered in each chapter meet the requirements of the National Curriculum for History.

The National Curriculum for History Programme of Study is covered in this book.

All pupils must study the following main topics.

- British History 1066–1500. (Chapter One.)
- British History 1500–1750 (Chapter Two.)
- British History 1750–1900. (Chapter Four.)
- A European study before 1914. (Chapter Three.)
- A world study before 1900. (Chapter Six.)
- A world study after 1900. (Chapter Five.)

History attainment targets

The Attainment Targets for History covers the following strands.

1 Knowledge and Understanding

This strand deals with Changes and Situations within history and Causes and Consequences of historical events. You learn about the most important individuals who influenced the course of events and who changed the way people behaved. Turning points in the history of a country or the world are also studied, since the world we live in today is linked to these events.

2 Historical Skills

This strand deals with ways of interpreting events and using a wide range of sources as historical evidence. Some sources are more valuable than other sources. Historians have to use a wide range of primary and secondary sources when they write about the past.

Citizenship

Citizenship themes are also covered in this book because the study of history helps you to understand what it is to be a citizen and to become aware of the rights and duties of being a citizen.

Literacy

The study of history should help you write coherently using key terms, well-structured sentences and organised paragraphs.

How this book will help

National Curriculum Levels

At the back of the book you will find the levels of response to questions on historical knowledge and skills questions. They are written in 'student speak'. Use this to assess which level you are reaching when you answer the questions in the end-of-chapter practice questions.

How this book is organised

The book is divided into six chapters which cover the six areas of the National Curriculum (see page 4). Every chapter is divided into sub chapters, to enable you to study each part of each theme in the National Curriculum.

To guide your study, we tell you at the start of the chapter what you should be able to understand. We do this in the box marked 'After studying this topic.'

In the book you will find the three main periods of British History, two world studies and a European Study. The **key points** and events are covered in each of the six chapters.

At the end of each topic you will find **Progress Checks**, which help you to test yourself on the key points of the topic.

Every chapter has a **narrative**, explaining the key events of the topic. There are also **extracts** written at the time of the period. These primary sources make the text come alive in a special way.

You will also see **pictures** and **maps** which will help you to understand the key events and behaviour of the people you are studying.

Spidergrams help to summarise the key points of the topics.

Margin notes add to the text and help to explain key points.

History is a very challenging and enjoyable subject. The book should help you to understand what you are studying at school and to practise the skills of using evidence and taking part in historical investigations.

The topics covered in this chapter are:

- Why did William of Normandy conquer England?
- William takes control of England
- The lives of the barons and knights
- Life in medieval villages
- The Christian Church and the people
- Towns in medieval England
- The people revolt against the lords
- England conquers Wales and not Scotland
- The growing power of Parliament

1.1 Why did William of Normandy conquer England?

After studying this topic you should be able to:

- identify which men wanted to become King of England in 1066
- understand why they thought they had a claim to the throne of England
- understand why William of Normandy won the English crown
- assess the characters of William and King Harold.

Three claimants to the throne

The phrase 'the Confessor' refers to the ancient Catholic practice of confessing one's sins to God, via a priest. Edward loved the Catholic Church.

The 'saintly King Edward' the 'Confessor' died on 5 January 1066 and there was a big struggle to become King of England after him.

- Earl Harold of Wessex, Edward's brother-in-law, England's leading nobleman and Edward's choice, was crowned on 6 January.

  A writer at the time tells us: *Earl Harold succeeded to the throne just as the King had granted it to him and as he had been chosen to the position. (Anglo-Saxon Chronicle, c 11th century)*

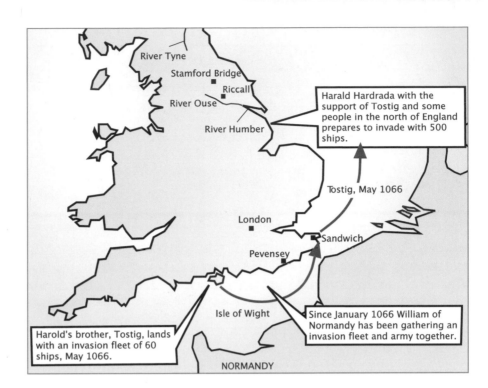

Fig. 1.1 Harold's problems, January to September 1066.

Map labels:
- River Tyne
- Stamford Bridge
- Riccall
- River Ouse
- River Humber
- Harald Hardrada with the support of Tostig and some people in the north of England prepares to invade with 500 ships.
- Tostig, May 1066
- London
- Sandwich
- Pevensey
- Isle of Wight
- Harold's brother, Tostig, lands with an invasion fleet of 60 ships, May 1066.
- Since January 1066 William of Normandy has been gathering an invasion fleet and army together.
- NORMANDY

Fig. 1.2 Harold promising the crown to William of Normandy.

- **King Harald Hardrada of Norway** said that Harthacnut, King of England in 1042, promised the crown to his family. He was supported by the King of Scotland and Harold's brother, Tostig.

  Harold finally defeated both of these men at the **Battle of Stamford Bridge** on **25 September 1066**.

- **William, Duke of Normandy**, said Edward had promised him the crown. In 1063 Edward gave William, whom he loved like a son, and whom he had already named his heir in 1051, a more serious pledge. He sent Harold to William to confirm his promise by oath. (William of Poitiers writing in 1073.)

William also told his followers that *Harold* had promised him the throne.

> *On the journey, Harold was in danger of being taken prisoner by Guy of Ponthieu. I rescued him by threat of war. Through his own hands he made himself my subject and gave me a firm pledge about the throne of England.* (quoted by William of Poitiers)

But Harold said that the oath had been made under pressure: he feared that he would have been kept in prison or killed if he had not taken the oath.

The Battle of Hastings

William took six months to prepare his armies to invade England and on **27 September 1066** he landed at Pevensey but rushed to **Hastings**, a better harbour from which to sail if he was defeated. He built a motte and bailey castle to make himself secure from attack.

Fig. 1.3 Preparing the invasion fleet.

Then William waited to fight Harold, who had gone to Yorkshire to defeat Hardrada and Tostig.

Key Point

There were three claimants to the throne after King Edward the Confessor had died. They were King Harold of England, King Harald of Norway and Duke William of Normandy. William actually won the throne and joined England to Normandy.

The **Battle of Hastings** took place on **14 October 1066**, and the Normans were victorious. Harold was killed and William became the most powerful man in England.

Fig. 1.4 Seeing his men fleeing, he took off his helmet and cried, '*Look at me well! I am still alive and by God's grace I shall yet prove victor.*'

A Norman observer of the Battle of Hastings wrote:

The English were as brave as we were. With their battle-axes and with men hurling spears and stones, they repelled our attacks and they killed many of our men shooting missiles from a distance. Indeed our men began to retreat; disobeying Harold's orders, the English footmen chased them from the field. It was only William's courage which saved us. … Fighting on foot he split shields, helmets and coats of mail with his great sword. Seeing his men fleeing, he took off his helmet and cried, 'Look at me well! I am still alive and by God's grace I shall yet prove victor.' This inspired his tired men who gathered for a final charge in which Harold was killed. Seeing this, the English fled as quickly as they could, leaving the bloodstained battleground. (William of Poitiers)

Remember Harold was fighting invasions on two fronts: in the north and in the south. He was a very brave fighter. He won the first battle in the north and nearly defeated William in the south.

In history, events occur for many reasons, not just one. Sometimes, as in 1066, luck plays a big part in historical events.

After the battle, William took his time getting to London where he was crowned on Christmas Day at Westminster Abbey. William built a wooden Tower of London as a refuge and stronghold and to warn the English that he was the powerful new ruler of the country.

William the Conqueror had won the English throne for many reasons.

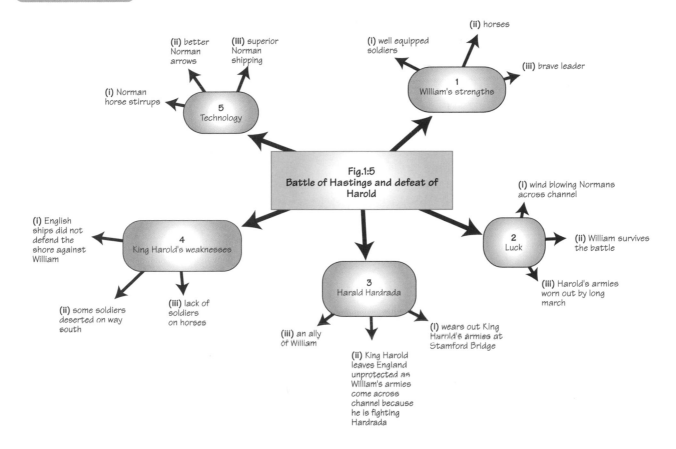

Fig.1:5 Battle of Hastings and defeat of Harold

1 William's strengths
- (i) well equipped soldiers
- (ii) horses
- (iii) brave leader

5 Technology
- (i) Norman horse stirrups
- (ii) better Norman arrows
- (iii) superior Norman shipping

4 King Harold's weaknesses
- (i) English ships did not defend the shore against William
- (ii) some soldiers deserted on way south
- (iii) lack of soldiers on horses

3 Harald Hardrada
- (i) wears out King Harold's armies at Stamford Bridge
- (ii) King Harold leaves England unprotected as William's armies come across channel because he is fighting Hardrada
- (iii) an ally of William

2 Luck
- (i) wind blowing Normans across channel
- (ii) William survives the battle
- (iii) Harold's armies worn out by long march

Progress Check

1 Who were the three men who claimed the English throne after King Edward died?
2 In what part of England is Stamford Bridge where King Harold won a victory?
3 Where did William of Normandy land in 1066?
4 What was the name of the famous battle when William defeated the English?
5 When and where was William crowned King of England?

1. Harold Godwinson, Harald Hardrada of Norway, William of Normandy. 2. The north of England. 3. Pevensey. 4. The Battle of Hastings. 5. Christmas Day 1066 in Westminster Abbey, London.

1.2 How did King William take control of England after the Battle of Hastings?

After studying this topic you should be able to:

- understand how William changed the way the land in England was organised
- describe how William crushed the people who rebelled against his rule
- appreciate the importance of the famous Domesday Book
- assess how successfully William organised England after he conquered it.

William needed to be careful after the Battle of Hastings because Harold's followers were angry at William's success – he had taken power in England for himself and his Norman followers.

An angry Saxon bishop wrote about William's success:

> *Such was the feebleness of the wretched people that after the first battle they never tried to rise up for their freedom. It was as though that when Harold fell so, too, fell the whole strength of the country.*

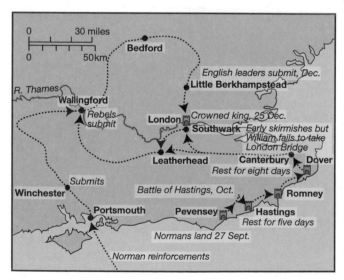

Fig. 1.6 March of the Norman army, October to December 1066.

Other English people refused to accept Norman rule and William had to cope with many rebellions from them. His barons and their knights travelled around England, killing the English rebels and taking away their land.

At the same time, William cleverly took many steps to take control of the lands of England.

1   He promised to follow 'saintly Edward's' **laws and customs**.

2   He was the **owner** of all the land in England, and directly controlled a quarter of it.

3   He allowed the **barons** to take over three-quarters of the land of the country as **tenants in chief**. They were to run the country on behalf of the King.

4   He and his Norman barons **built castles** from which they imposed their rule on the surrounding areas.

5   His barons had to swear the '**Oath of Salisbury**' because William knew

that the barons might become too powerful in their own castles and that the followers of these barons might follow them and not obey the King. *I become your man from this day forward, for life and limb and loyalty. I shall be true and faithful to you for the lands I hold from you.*

The Domesday Book

William decided to find out exactly what went on in his kingdom. His followers surveyed the country and wrote the famous **Domesday Book**. His officers gave him hundreds of pages of sheepskin, sewn together to form a book, which contained all the details he had asked for.

An English monk wrote about the compiling of the Domesday Book:

> *He had a record made of how much land his archbishop had, and his bishops, abbots, earls ... what or how much everybody had who occupied land in England, in land or cattle, and how much money it was worth. There was not a hide of land, ox or cow or pig left out of his record.* (Anglo-Saxon Chronicle)

The feudal system

William and the Norman kings imposed the **feudal system** on England, to organise the way that **land** was looked after.

The feudal system described the way in which owners of land (king, nobles, churchmen and peasants) were linked to one another. William kept about a quarter of the land for himself. The rest was divided up among his followers, called barons or 'tenants in chief', to whom the King was in fact lending the land in return for their loyalty and service.

Fig. 1.7 Castles of the Norman conquest at the end of the 12th century.

Under the Feudal system, the King was really the owner of all the land in England. His barons were lent land in return for obedience to him. In turn the barons lent land to the knights in return for their obedience. The peasants also had to obey the knights and barons in return for living and working on the land.

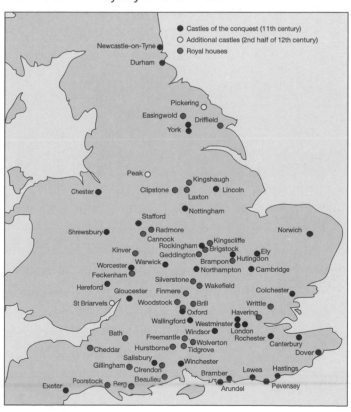

William showed that he was a very cunning ruler in the way he organised the land of England.

William knew that his more powerful followers (barons) might rebel in spite of oaths of loyalty. So while he gave these 200 men large amounts of land, he made sure their holdings were divided up, with, for example, one baron owning land in Wiltshire, Middlesex, Hertfordshire, Sussex and Surrey. This kept the barons travelling around their estates and made it hard for them to raise a rebel army.

> **Key Point** William of Normandy's conquest shows that he and his followers were good organisers.

Rebellions crushed

William dealt ruthlessly with rebellions.

The legend of Robin Hood was based on true events – stories of Saxon rebellions against the Norman invaders.

- In 1067 one of his barons, Eustace of Boulogne, sided with a Saxon rising in Kent. William's army destroyed the rebels.
- In 1068 he crushed rebellions in Devon and Gloucester, and defeated the Saxon earls Edwin and Morcar – but when they surrendered to him, he allowed them to keep their land.
- In 1069 Edgar of the old line of Wessex kings joined King Swein of Denmark in a Northern rebellion. William took two years to put down this rising, destroying most of the northern counties as he did so.

A Norman description of William's treatment of the north is evidence of William's harshness:

> *The royal forces approached York, only to learn that the Danes had fled. … He cut down many in his vengeance; and harried the land, and burned homes to ashes. Nowhere else had William shown such cruelty. He made no effort to control his fury and punished the innocent with the guilty. In his anger he ordered that all crops, herds and food of every kind should be brought together and burned to ashes. One hundred thousand folk of both sexes, young and old alike, perished of hunger.* (Roger Wace)

Changes to the Feudal system

The feudal system did not stay exactly the same throughout the Middle Ages (see topics 1.4 and 1.7) but England continued to be ruled by the monarchy. Some kings were very good at controlling the system and others were not. The feudal system depended on the King being very strong.

The barons, including some abbots, were still the most powerful people after the king. Some barons became richer and more powerful than other barons if they were good organisers and fighters, and the kings often found it difficult to control them

Weak kings like King Stephen were unable to control the barons, and this led to **chaos and civil war**.

Under the barons were the **knights**, who served the barons and fought under them for the King whenever the King demanded it. Many knights also became richer during the Middle Ages, buying and selling land and trading with townspeople, so they became more difficult to control.

The **peasants** were the poorest people in medieval England, under the control of barons and knights. They had no power. Most English nobles were pushed down into the peasant class.

> The conquest of England by the Normans was a key turning point in English history, because a new ruling class took over England. The country was now joined up with Europe.

Progress Check

1 What was the name of the book that William ordered to be written to show who owned what in England?
2 Name the system by which William and the Norman kings controlled the land in England.
3 Where and when did the barons of England swear to obey the King?
4 Give another name for the barons.
5 Name the baron who rebelled against William's rule in 1067.
6 How did William decide to divide up the land among the barons?

1. The Domesday Book. 2. The feudal system. 3. Salisbury, 1086. 4. Tenants in Chief. 5. Eustace of Boulogne. 6. He gave each baron lands in various places around the country.

1.3 What was life like for the barons and the knights in the Middle Ages?

After studying this topic you should be able to:

● **say why the Normans built castles when they came to England**
● **understand what life was like in these castles**
● **describe how they changed over time**
● **understand how castles were attacked and defended**
● **appreciate what becoming a knight involved**
● **describe the main aspects of the life of a knight.**

Barons in their castles

The defeated Saxons were forced to build William's first castle at Hastings, as a place of retreat if he was attacked by the defeated Saxons.

Fig. 1.8 Digging the ditch for William's first castle at Hastings.

They dug a large circular ditch, throwing the earth up to form a **mound** (**motte**). On top they built a fort from timbers brought in by the invasion fleet, and they dug a ditch to enclose a larger area (**bailey**) where, later, they put huts for castle servants, a blacksmith's forge, chapel, bakery and so on.

Around the motte and bailey castle, they put a wooden fence for protection. A wooden bridge linked the motte and the bailey.

 Key Point

You should note that castles were symbols of authority for barons as well as the King. They also developed over time, as technology improved.

William's barons built similar castles on their new estates in case they were attacked by the Saxons, and by 1070 about 400 had been built. Later, when they felt safe, the barons replaced their wooden castles with stone ones. Wooden ones could more easily be set on fire by an enemy, and, in any case, wood got wet and eventually rotted.

The first stone castles were fairly simple. The tower was called a **keep** since people kept their goods there. Its walls could be more than three metres thick. Inside there were few rooms and little comfort: the damp air and winds came through the narrow slits (**windy eyes**) making the stone building even colder.

Fig. 1.9 A cross-section of a stone keep.

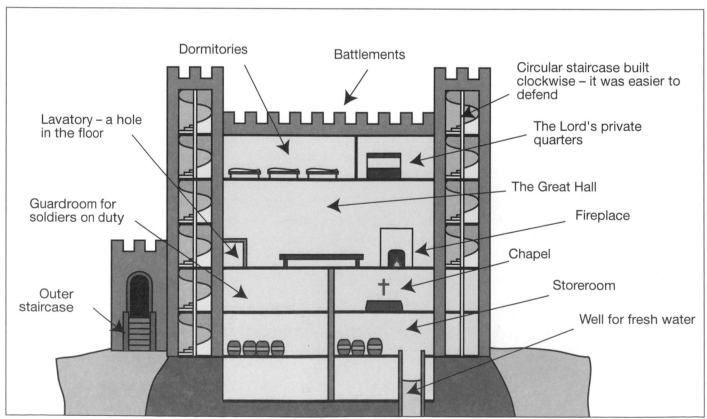

Dormitories

Battlements

Circular staircase built clockwise – it was easier to defend

Lavatory – a hole in the floor

The Lord's private quarters

The Great Hall

Guardroom for soldiers on duty

Fireplace

Chapel

Outer staircase

Storeroom

Well for fresh water

Fig. 1.10 An artist's impression of attackers using a belfry.

Later castles were much larger and had **stone defensive walls** around the castle area. The walls had defensive **towers**, which became more rounded and more difficult to attack as builders became more skilled.

Castles were **easy to defend** as long as food and water lasted. Defenders could fire from the top of the castle walls, with arrows, stones or burning tar. They could see their attackers coming from a long way off, because castles were built on hills or near rivers.

Attackers used various methods to try to break down walls. A wheeled **belfry** put across a filled-in moat allowed miners to dig beneath the walls. They then filled the dug-out area with wood, which was lit to dry out the mortar holding the stones together and make the wall collapse. The defenders had the easier task, sheltered by the castle walls.

Key Point
- Castles were the main method of control of England under the Normans.
- They developed over time.
- Remains of these castles are in many places in the country.

How King Stephen captured Exeter Castle in 1136, according to an eyewitness

Its castle is on a high mound protected by towers of stone and strong walls. Inside, Baldwin had a strong garrison to man the walls and towers. They taunted the King and his men as they approached the walls. They made some unexpected sorties and fell upon the royal army. At other times they shot arrows and threw missiles from above. The King used miners to dig under the fortifications. He had all types of machines built, some of great height, others level with the foot of the walls to batter them down. (Adapted from a writer at the time)

How barons and knights learned and loved to fight

The Norman kings gave large parts of their land to their more important followers, the barons. The barons gave parts of their landholdings to some of their followers called knights. In return for his land, a knight had to spend 40 days every year in the king's army, bringing his own horse, weapons and band of foot soldiers. These foot soldiers were often English.

The **Bayeux Tapestry** shows servants carrying the armour of the knight. The armour was very heavy, since it was made out of iron rings linked together. It was called chain mail.

Fig. 1.11
Knights in armour in the Bayeux Tapestry.

The Bayeux Tapestry was a strip cartoon sewn in wool by English needlewomen on the orders of William's Bishop Odo of Bayeux, which still hangs in Bayeux, France, today.

Later on, as craftsmen became more skilled, armour improved and the whole body was covered by a metal suit. Some suits of armour weighed about 30 kg, so knights' horses had to be powerful animals. The knights' main weapons were the **lance** – a long thin spear – and the **sword**. Later on, knights had very well-developed and strong metal lances. On their shields, each knight had his own badge (or **coat of arms**) which was designed and coloured by important officials called **heralds**.

The knight's main **feudal duty** was to fight his lord's enemies. He knew that he might die in battle, but he also knew that he was much more likely to be captured if his lord's side lost a battle.

Knights' sons were prepared from an early age to become knights themselves. At seven years of age they were sent to live in another nobleman's castle. They had to be his personal servant and the lord taught the page how to behave, wear armour, ride and use a sword and lance.

At the age of 15 the page became a **squire**.

Fig. 1.12 Arming a young knight. The King ties the knight's sword at his belt while the squire puts on the knight's spurs.

A tournament at Smithfield in 1390, as described by Jean Froissart in 1390

On Sunday afternoon sixty decorated war horses, each ridden by a squire, processed out of London. Following them came sixty noble ladies riding highly decorated ponies, each leading a knight in armour. This procession moved through London to Smithfield where the Queen of England, her ladies, as well as the King were waiting. … When the tournament began many were unhorsed, and many more lost their helmets. The joust went on until night came. Then everyone went to the feast.

Becoming a knight

Stages of becoming a knight:
stage one – page;
stage two – squire;
stage three – knight.

The knights became the most important 'middle class' of the country; they became MPs (see chapter 2).

When he was 21 a squire could become a knight if his lord or the King decided that he was fully prepared. The young man spent the night before his knighting in prayer (the **vigil**). He was supposed to think about his knightly duties – to be kind to women in particular and to everyone in general, to be brave and honest, to be loyal to his lord and King, and to be gentle.

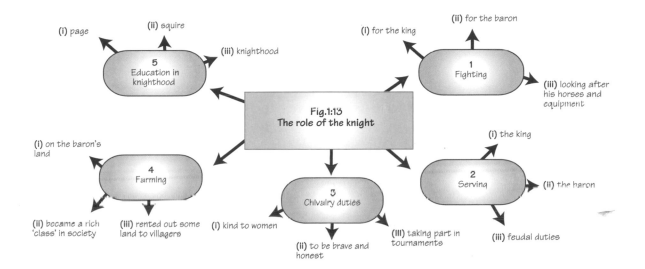

Fig.1:13
The role of the knight

5 Education in knighthood
(i) page
(ii) squire
(iii) knighthood

1 Fighting
(i) for the king
(ii) for the baron
(iii) looking after his horses and equipment

4 Farming
(i) on the baron's land
(ii) became a rich 'class' in society
(iii) rented out some land to villagers

3 Chivalry duties
(i) kind to women
(ii) to be brave and honest
(iii) taking part in tournaments

2 Serving
(i) the king
(ii) the baron
(iii) feudal duties

Key Point

The knight's life was focused on warfare.
The word 'chivalry' comes from the French word for horse.

When a king wanted to fight a **long war in Europe**, he needed followers who would stay longer than the 40 days' service which his knights owed him. So, from the 13th century onwards, kings began to allow knights to pay them **shield money** (or **scutage**, from the Latin for shield) instead of serving for 40 days. This gave kings enough money to pay those knights who were willing to serve for as long as a war lasted.

Progress Check

1 To whom did the barons give part of their land?
2 Who had given the barons their land?
3 Before a boy became a knight, what was his title?
4 Who did a knight promise to serve?
5 What was a knight's armour made of?
6 In what buildings did the Norman barons live?

1. Knights. 2. The King. 3. Squire. 4. The baron or the King. 5. Iron. 6. Castles.

1.4 What was life like in the villages of medieval England?

After studying this topic you should understand:

- how the barons' land was divided up
- what life on the manor was like for villagers
- how the lord of the manor lived
- the effects of the Black Death
- how feudalism began to die.

Over time knights became rich through trade and farming. Their lands were called **manors**, where people produced almost everything they needed. The manor houses were stone built with a large hall and a grand table.

The description below by an owner of a manor gives us an idea of the lives of peasants.

> Villeins were people living in villages.

> *The villeins each had a virgate of land (about 14 acres), for which they had to plough, sow and till half an acre of the lord's desmesne: they had also to give such services as the lord's bailiff would demand, pay a quarter of seed-wheat at Michaelmas, a peck of wheat, four bushels of oats and three hens on 12 November, and at Christmas a cock, two hens and two-penn'orth of bread.*
> (Quoted in Upper Class, P. Lane, 1972)

The following famous poem tells us about the meals the lord of the manor ate.

> *His bread, his ale were finest of the fine*
> *And no one had a better stock of wine.*
> *His house was never short of bake-meat pies,*
> *…*
> *Many a bream and pike were in his pond.*
> *And in his hall a table stood arrayed*
> *All ready all day long, with places laid.*
> (Geoffrey Chaucer, 1340–1400)

Villagers' houses were small. The single room on the ground floor had a partition behind which animals were kept – a cow or two, a couple of pigs, chickens and so on. They had **little furniture** – wooden dishes, a cooking pot and a few simple stools.

For the villagers, the basic food was **black bread** which they had for breakfast at sunrise, for dinner at 10.00 am (with cheese or eggs) and for supper at 4.00 pm (with soup or stew). For most of the year they ate salted meat, mainly bacon from their pigs. Unlike the lord, villagers often had little to eat, and if there was a bad harvest, many died of starvation.

Fig. 1.14 Entertainers and musicians would perform for guests at castles and manor houses – particularly at festival times.

Hard work on the farm

Manor farms consisted of three huge fields, common land and the surrounding forest. Each field went through a **three-year cycle**. In year one it grew wheat or rye, in year two oats or barley, and in year three it was left unploughed (fallow) to give the land a chance to recover.

Villagers were given **strips of land** for their own use. Each field was split into strips of about 200 metres by 20 metres and each villager had a number of strips in different parts of each field.

The villagers' year was a seasonal one. In the spring the the soil was prepared. Sowing of seed was done by men carrying bags of seed which they threw out by hand. In the autumn, came harvesting. Then, when the corn ears had been flailed from the straw, each villager took their corn to be ground. Villagers hated paying the lord for the use of the mill.

Fig. 1.15 The three-field system, Wigston Magna, Leicestershire.

Fig. 1.17 Carrying corn to the mill.

Fig. 1.16 Rotation of the three-field system.

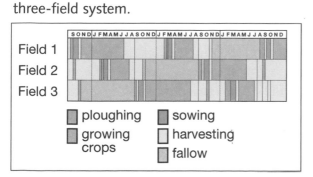

	S O N D	J F M A M J J A S O N D	J F M A M J J A S O N D	J F M A M J J A S O N D
Field 1				
Field 2				
Field 3				

☐ ploughing ☐ sowing
☐ growing crops ☐ harvesting
☐ fallow

Fig. 1.18 A two-oxened plough.

The ploughman's words explain what life on the farm was like.

> *I work very hard. At dawn I drive the oxen in the field and yoke them to the plough. However harsh the winter, I dare not stay at home, for fear of my lord. Every day I have to plough an acre or more. I have a boy who drives the oxen with a goad, and he is always hoarse from cold and shouting. I fill the ox-bins with hay and water, and I clear out the dung.*
> (Said to Aelfric, Abbot of Eynsham, 1066)

Disease and hardship were common, as stated by this English observer in 1131.

> *In that year there was such a great animal plague as had never been before. It affected cattle and pigs; in a village that had 10 or 12 ploughs in action there was not one left.* (Anglo-Saxon Chronicle)

Ploughman and shepherds had very strict rules for their work, according to Fleta, a writer in 1170.

> *The art of the ploughman is in knowing how to make a straight furrow with the oxen. … They must feed their animals, sleep with them at night, rub them down, make sure their food is not stolen. … Shepherds should be intelligent, watchful and kind men who will not harry the sheep by their bad temper … should have a good barking dog and sleep with their sheep at night.*

Changing country life – the Black Death

By 1300 the population was three times greater than in 1066. To produce **more food**, parts of **forests were cleared** and **marshes were drained**. Increased demand for cloth exports led to an **increased demand for wool**.

The **Black Death** brought chaos and death to English villages. In 1348 the people of England were attacked by a plague brought from abroad by black rats infected with plague-carrying fleas. People found large lumps under their armpits and their bodies covered with red and black spots (hence the 'Black Death'). The Black Death was also spread through germs that people breathed in. **One-third of the population died.** Some places were left with no inhabitants.

Henry Knighton wrote at the time (1363) about life in England.

> *In the parish of Holy Cross more than 400 died. After the pestilence many buildings fell into ruins in every borough and village, for lack of people; many places became deserted, all having died who lived there.*

Fig. 1.19 Praying for a plague victim.

Some thought the disease was caused by the smell from diseased people. They hoped to be saved by carrying flowers. Some people prayed that God would save them from death.

Wages rose because the lords of the manor had fewer workers to do all the jobs on the farm. Parliament passed laws to try to stop wages from rising and to stop villagers from moving to new manors. These laws did not work very well, since lords of the manor had to offer higher wages to pay for all the work that needed to be done.

The decline of feudalism during the Middle Ages

In the 13th century, kings started to demand money from the barons instead of making them send knights when there was a war in Europe to fight. The kings then paid money to full-time soldiers, called mercenaries.

Key Point

Life in the medieval village was harsh.
The Middle Ages saw many changes in village life.

The higher wages after the Black Death also freed people from feudalism, since with money in their pockets, ordinary people had more choices.

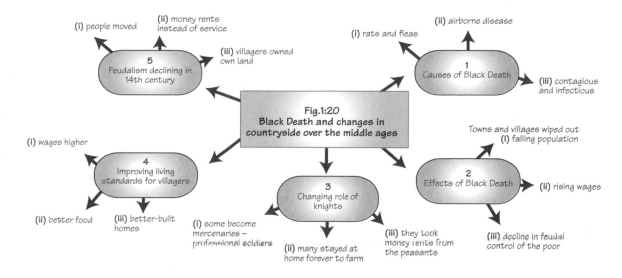

5 Feudalism declining in 14th century
(i) people moved
(ii) money rents instead of service
(iii) villagers owned own land

1 Causes of Black Death
(i) rats and fleas
(ii) airborne disease
(iii) contagious and infectious

Fig.1:20 Black Death and changes in countryside over the middle ages

4 Improving living standards for villagers
(i) wages higher
(ii) better food
(iii) better-built homes

3 Changing role of knights
(i) some become mercenaries – professional soldiers
(ii) many stayed at home forever to farm
(iii) they took money rents from the peasants

2 Effects of Black Death
Towns and villages wiped out
(i) falling population
(ii) rising wages
(iii) decline in feudal control of the poor

Progress Check

1 What was the name given to the land owned by a baron?
2 How many fields were there in a manor farm?
3 How was the villagers' land divided up?
4 What was the name of the plague that struck England in 1348?
5 What did Parliament try to do about the wages of the villagers?
6 What happened to feudalism during the Middle Ages?

1. Manor. 2. Three. 3. Into strips. 4. The Black Death. 5. Stop them rising. 6. It declined.

1.5 How did the Christian Church affect the lives of the people in the Middle Ages?

After studying this topic you should be able to:

● appreciate how important religion was in the Middle Ages
● understand how the Church was organised
● understand why monasteries were built and how monks lived
● appreciate why many people criticised the Church
● understand the reasons and the effects of Henry II's quarrel with the Church.

Bishops and their cathedrals

Religion was very important to people in England during the Middle Ages. It is sometimes difficult for people today to appreciate this. The Church was the centre of the lives of ordinary people.

Medieval kings wanted the Catholic Church to help keep the country peaceful, as can be seen by the following account from the time:

> *The priest should ask the peasants whether they have cheated by not paying their full tithes to the church; whether they have been obedient to their lord; whether they have done all the work they should for the lord; whether they have broken into a neighbour's land with plough or animal.* (From a handbook for the medieval clergy, c 1380)

William I brought men from France to become bishops and abbots. They were great landowners and barons, so they controlled hundreds of knights, and they were really **agents of the King**. The Bishop of Durham guarded the northern border with Scotland. The Archbishop of Canterbury was the

The King and the Church supported each other in keeping authority over the people.

Fig. 1.21 The nave of Durham Cathedral.

first man of the Kingdom as the leader of the Church in England. He controlled a great deal of land.

The country was divided into a number of **dioceses**, each with its bishop, with the Archbishop of Canterbury as the leader of the Church in England. Dioceses were divided into **parishes** with their own parish church and parish priest. Bishops set up schools in their dioceses and made sure that the teachers taught what the Church, the King and lords wanted people to learn.

Each bishop had his seat in his own church (or **cathedral**). The first cathedrals, built in the 11th century, copied the Roman style and are known as **Romanesque**. They had thick walls, massive columns, round arches and few windows.

Bishops ruled their dioceses and estates, and helped to run the country as government ministers or ambassadors. Some had too little time for Church work and some of their priests became greedy and lazy. Such behaviour was attacked by the writer Chaucer in The Canterbury Tales, by rebels in the Peasants' Revolt and by the Lollards, early Protestants who thought the Church leaders should live according to the standards of the Bible.

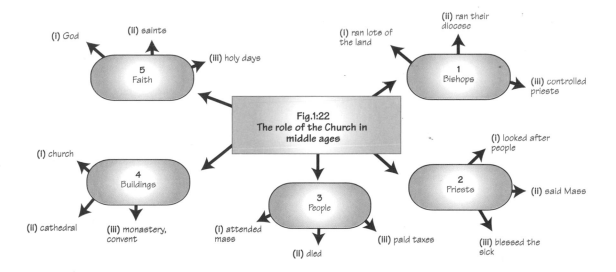

Monasteries and convents

Monasteries and convents were at the centre of life for Christians in England. Men and women who wanted a strict life of prayer and hard work, dedicated to God, went to live in monasteries (where men became monks) and convents (where women became nuns). Hundreds of such communities were set up in England after 1066. By 1300, there were over 600 monasteries and the same number of convents in England.

Wedding ceremonies and funerals of members of the royal family often take place at Westminster Abbey.

Fig. 1.23 A statue of a monk.

They were often built in a sheltered valley, the stream providing water for kitchens, a washing place and a system for taking away sewage.

The most important building was the church. Many of these became our most well-known cathedrals, such as Salisbury Cathedral and Winchester Cathedral.

The cloister was the covered passageway, where the monks read, heard lectures and wrote books. Meals were taken in silence.

Often, the monasteries and convents were built using money given by a rich baron or the King, as a way of giving glory to God and ensuring their place in heaven. Villagers also paid a great percentage of their money towards the building of the monasteries.

Provided he was at least 16 years old, a person could take vows of **poverty** (he would own nothing), **chastity** (or purity), **obedience** (to superiors) and **stability** (to stay in the same monastery for life).

A novice wrote about his hard but peaceful life at Rivaulx Abbey in 1239:

> *Our food is scanty, our clothes rough; our drink is from the stream and our sleep often on our book. Under tired limbs there is only a mat; when sleep is sweetest we must rise at the bell's call. But everywhere is peace and serenity.*

Monks prayed six times a day in the church: at 2.00 am (matins), 7.00 am (prime), 9.00 am (tierce, or third prayer), 12.00 noon (sext), 5.00 pm (vespers, or evening prayer) and 7.00 pm (compline, or final prayer).

However, during the Middle Ages many monks began to abandon the life of hard work as shown by the following extract.

> *He described with relish the number of well-cooked dishes and sauces he had eaten with the monks at Canterbury. He had no appetite left, he said, for the main course of vegetables, and he praised also the wine, mead and fruit juice that went with the meal.*

Key Point

Religion was a central part of life in the Middle Ages.
Most people believed in God and the Catholic Church.

The murder of the Archbishop of Canterbury in 1162

Many people went on pilgrimages to places linked to their faith, such as Canterbury, as famously described by Geoffrey Chaucer in *The Prologue* to his *The Canterbury Tales*.

*Then people long to go on pilgrimages
And palmers long to see the stranger strands
Of far off saints, hallowed in sundry lands,
And specially, from every shire's end
In England, down to Canterbury they wend.*

(The Canterbury Tales, c 1390)

In Chapter 2 you will find out how King Henry VIII got complete control of the Church.

Thomas à Becket, the Archbishop of Canterbury, was killed by some knights of King Henry II. King Henry II was trying to widen his power as King and tried to take over the church courts and to control who became bishops, rather than allowing the Pope to appoint them.

Becket **excommunicated** Henry and his supporters, cutting them off from the Church's life, a serious matter in Catholic England.

As this source written by a modern historian shows, Henry's anger led to murder.

Fig. 1.24 Becket defying Henry.

His anger burst through and he shouted words he was always after to regret. 'What knaves have I fed in my house that they are faithless to their lord, and let him be tricked so infamously by one upstart clerk.

Becket's murder was then carried out by the knights, according to an eyewitness.

The knights called out, 'Where is Thomas Becket, traitor to the King?' His voice said, 'I am here, no traitor to the King, but a priest.' 'You shall die,' they cried. 'I am ready to die for my Lord, so long as the Church can have its freedom.'

Find out who the Archbishop of Canterbury is today.

The King walked to Canterbury to the place where Becket had been assassinated. As a penance for his sin, he walked barefoot. Becket was made a saint and a shrine was made to remember him, but the shrine was later destroyed on the orders of King Henry VIII in 1533.

Fig. 1.25 The murder of Thomas à Becket.

Voices for and against the Church

The manorial (or parish) church was the largest building in the village or town in the Middle Ages, after the castle or manorial hall.

Fig. 1.26 Parish church of St John at Wicken, Northamptonshire.

In 1086 Norwich, for example, had 1000 houses, 20 churches and 40 chapels.

The Church had an **important part in medieval life**. On Sundays and 100 **holy days** (holidays) the Church banned working; everyone went to Mass on those days, and learned about their faith from wall paintings. Biblical stories were shown in stained glass windows. Churches were often built on a hill so that people could go there if there was a flood. They could see the church at dawn and at dusk.

There were some **good priests** in the Middle Ages. Geoffrey Chaucer wrote about one particular good priest:

> *A holy-minded man whose good was known*
> *There was, and poor, the parson of a town.*
> *Indeed, he much liked beyond any doubt,*
> *To give to poor parishioners all about,*
> *From his own goods and gifts at Eastertide*
> *(The Canterbury Tales, c 1390)*

But Langland's description of an 'unworthy priest' gives a different account.

> *I have been priest and parson for thirty winters past.*
> *But I can find a hare in a field or in a furrow*
> *Better than construe the first Psalm or explain it to the parish.*
> *I can hold a friendly meeting. I can cast a shire's accounts,*
> *But in mass-book or Pope's edict I cannot read a line.*
> (From Piers the Ploughman, by William Langland, c 1370)

Key Point

Different viewpoints in primary sources are useful to historians because we learn that there were different views at the time. A 'biased' source therefore can be a valuable source.

Fig. 1.27 John Wycliff.

John Wycliff, a priest at Oxford, attacked the lives of worldly bishops, greedy monks and ignorant priests. People called him a lollard, a slang word for complainer. His followers were then also called **Lollards**. Many craftsmen as well as Oxford lecturers supported him. In 1381 he was driven from Oxford because he attacked the Church's teaching on the Eucharist. Wycliff died in 1384.

Lollards complained about unworthy priests, as this source tells us:

> *At Leicester a priest called William of Swynderby preached against the clergy saying they were bad, and, as other Lollards said ... to pay evil clergy was to agree with their wickedness. The Bishop heard about this and banned William from preaching.*
> (Chronicles, Henry Knighton, c 1395)

A long-term cause of change may be compared to when a rolling snowball turns into an avalanche. These criticisms of the church gradually grew in some parts of England and led to the **Reformation** (see Chapter 2).

Parliament passed a law for the **burning of heretics**. MPs knew that an attack on the Church was also an attack on the King.

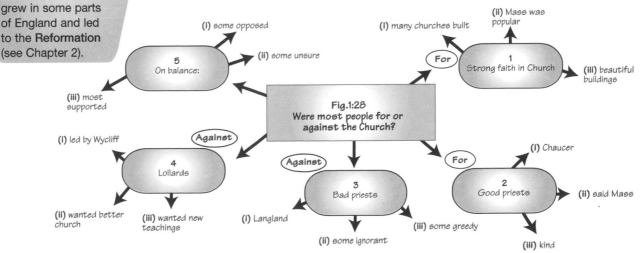

Fig.1:28 Were most people for or against the Church?

1 Strong faith in Church — For
(i) many churches built
(ii) Mass was popular
(iii) beautiful buildings

2 Good priests — For
(i) Chaucer
(ii) said Mass
(iii) kind

3 Bad priests — Against
(i) Langland
(ii) some ignorant
(iii) some greedy

4 Lollards — Against
(i) led by Wycliff
(ii) wanted better church
(iii) wanted new teachings

5 On balance:
(i) some opposed
(ii) some unsure
(iii) most supported

1.6 Why were towns in medieval England so important?

After studying this topic you should be able to:

- **explain why towns grew in the Middle Ages**
- **understand what life was like in these towns**
- **appreciate the roles of merchants and craftsmen in towns**
- **understand the role of the guilds**
- **explain the importance of the Town Charter.**

People in villages (see topic 1.4) travelled to towns to trade, and sometimes moved there to live.

The Domesday Book named over 100 small towns. Towns grew as **ports**, **river crossings** and **market centres**. During the 12th and 13th centuries over 140 new towns were built. Some grew around **castles**, **cathedrals** and **monasteries**, which employed craftsmen; some were built by **landowners**.

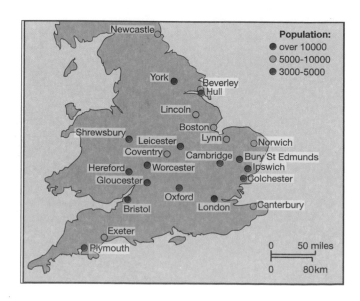

Fig. 1.29 Main English towns in the late 14th century.

An Italian's view of London in 1497 gives a very useful account of town life.

> *It is defended by handsome walls on the northern side. Within these is a strongly defended castle on the banks of the river where the King lives. There is a beautiful bridge which has on it many shops of stone and even a large church. The streets are so badly paved that they get wet whenever it rains, or when the water slops from the buckets being carried by animals. Then evil-smelling mud lasts nearly the year round.* (*Itinerarium Britanniae*, by Andreas Franciscus)

Towns often had toll gates, which were opened at dawn to allow in 'foreigners' coming to market, and closed again at sunset when 'foreigners' had to leave. In the towns were craftsmen who made things and merchants who sold things and who united in a **merchant guild** (or society).

Rich merchants often tried to get the Church, the King or the landowner to sell them a charter to allow them to run the town themselves. Many towns received these charters and became free from the control of King, Church and baron.

Fig. 1.30 A blacksmith in the 12th century.

The Normans saw England as a wealthy country because of the towns, as this source tells us.

> *England is a land which is fertile and rich because of the wealth which its merchants have increased by bringing in riches.* (Quoted in *Historical Atlas of Britain*, by Falkus and Gillingham, 1981)

Goldsmiths, blacksmiths, butchers and bakers were common jobs in towns.

Craftsmen worked in the towns, making things for merchants to sell. People doing the same craft lived near one another, and so names of medieval streets read like a list of occupations – Baker Street, Butchers' Row and so on.

Fig. 1.31 In the workroom and shop.

The **noise** from the workrooms and from the traders shouting added to the confusion caused by cattle, horses and donkeys. Blood from slaughter-houses and butchers' shops, fish heads from fishmongers made streets **dangerous** and **dirty**.

Like the merchants, craftsmen had their own **guilds**, one for each craft. Guild officers collected money each week so that members were looked after at times of sickness.

A boy might become an **apprentice** to a master craftsman who would teach him the 'mysteries' of the craft. After about seven years as an apprentice, guild officers allowed him to become a journeyman – a person paid by the day (*journée* in French). He then trained to be a craftsman.

On important religious holy days, the craftsmen and journeymen worked together to produce plays based on Bible stories. These 'mystery plays' were stopped in the Protestant Reformation (see Chapter 2).

Fig. 1.32 A craftsman who had been selling goods at too high a profit, in the pillory, a form of punishment.

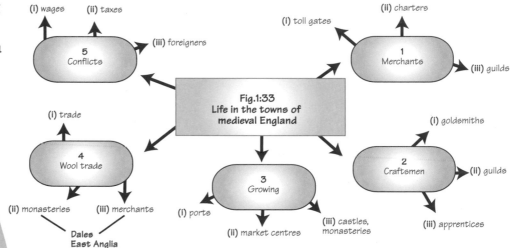

Fig.1:33 Life in the towns of medieval England

5 Conflicts — (i) wages — (ii) taxes — (iii) foreigners

1 Merchants — (i) toll gates — (ii) charters — (iii) guilds

4 Wool trade — (i) trade — (ii) monasteries — (iii) merchants — Dales East Anglia

3 Growing — (i) ports — (ii) market centres — (iii) castles, monasteries

2 Craftsmen — (i) goldsmiths — (ii) guilds — (iii) apprentices

Notice that in the Middle Ages, town life was different from village life. People had different experiences of life according to where they lived.

Key Point
- Life in the medieval town was different from village life.
- There were more opportunities in the towns and the towns grew over time.
- The people who led the towns were very powerful.

Fig. 1.34 Spinning.

Many towns became rich from the **wool trade**.

For many centuries England's **main export** was **wool**, highly valued by cloth-makers in Flanders, Germany and Italy. The main sheep-rearing areas were the Cotswolds, East Anglia and the southwest. Manorial lords, especially those in the great abbeys, earned huge sums from their sale of wool.

After the sheep had been sheared, the wool was put into packs and taken to the nearest market town. It was gathered into large sacks, which were stamped by one of the **Merchants of the Staple**, appointed by kings.

Progress Check

1 Name the book that listed 100 towns in England.
2 Which organisations did merchants and craftsmen form?
3 What was a journeyman?
4 Before becoming a craftsman, what did a boy have to do?
5 What did merchants try to buy for their town?
6 What product did many towns grow rich on?

1. The Domesday Book. 2. Guilds. 3. A worker paid by the day. 4. Serve an apprenticeship. 5. A charter. 6. Wool.

1.7 Why did people revolt against the lords in 1381?

After studying this topic you should be able to:

- **understand the causes of the Peasants' Revolt**
- **evaluate the importance of these causes**
- **explain how the Revolt spread**
- **appreciate how the Revolt was crushed**
- **understand the effects of the Revolt.**

The reasons behind the Peasants' Revolt

The **feudal system** had begun to decay in the 12th century, but landowners and Parliament tried to turn back the clock by enforcing feudal duties and limiting the wages of workers, who were able to demand higher pay after the Black Death.

Ex-soldiers' discontent also grew, since many ordinary people played an important part in the victories over the French in the battles of **Crecy** and **Agincourt**, as is seen by the following quotation.

They made all France afraid. And although they are not called 'Master' as gentlemen are, or 'Sir' as knights are, but only 'John' and 'Thomas' and so on, yet they have been found to have done great deeds at Crecy and Poitiers.
(Quoted in Illustrated History of England, by G R Trevelyan, 1926)

Soldiers had grown in **self-confidence** and **wealth** and the trials of rebels in 1381-2 showed that many of them farmed as much as 200 acres. They were unwilling to be pushed around by a landowners' Parliament. Other former soldiers had become **prosperous craftsmen in chartered boroughs**. They, too, resented attempts by landowners to win back feudal dues. This helps to explain why the people of London opened the city gates to the rebels in 1381.

There was **religious discontent** too. Many people, including some landowners, were angered by the over-rich bishops, abbots and monks (see topic 1.6).

For these reasons, many people supported the preaching of reforming priests such as **John Ball** and the arguments of men like **Wat Tyler**, who talked about equality for all.

The **immediate cause** of the uprising was **taxation**. In 1377 the French landed an army on the Isle of Wight and their navy attacked towns along the coast of southern England. To respond to this the government needed extra taxes to pay for larger armies. The first **poll tax** came in 1377: everybody over the age of 15 had to pay 4 pence. There was another such tax in 1379 and a third in 1381, when the tax was 12 pence per person.

This was the spark which lit the fire of revolt. Many people hid in the forests to escape the tax collectors: others fought the tax collectors. Then, in April 1381, the Chancellor, Archbishop Sudbury, was allowed to send armed forces to compel people to pay the tax. The Peasants' Revolt followed.

> The Peasants' Revolt is a good example of how important events are brought about by a variety of causes. There is never one cause. Never start an answer about why an event happened with a sentence like: 'The Revolt happened because...' It is much better to write: 'There were many reasons for the Revolt. One was...'.

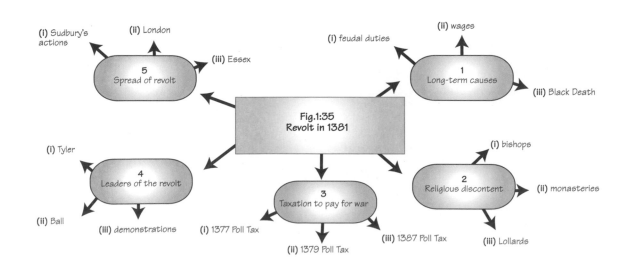

(i) Sudbury's actions   **(ii)** London   **(iii)** Essex
5 Spread of revolt

(i) feudal duties   **(ii)** wages   **(iii)** Black Death
1 Long-term causes

Fig.1:35 Revolt in 1381

(i) Tyler   **(ii)** Ball   **(iii)** demonstrations
4 Leaders of the revolt

(i) 1377 Poll Tax   **(ii)** 1379 Poll Tax   **(iii)** 1387 Poll Tax
3 Taxation to pay for war

(i) bishops   **(ii)** monasteries   **(iii)** Lollards
2 Religious discontent

Key Point

- The 1381 Peasants' Revolt shocked the nobles and the King.
- Anger about religion, wages, working conditions, war and taxation, together with good leaders, all played their part in starting the Revolt.

The story of the Peasants' Revolt

A chronology of the event shows how quickly the trouble spread.

> **The course of the Peasants' Revolt, 1381**
>
> **7 June**: Wat Tyler led Kentish rebels at Maidstone and marched on London.
>
> **12 June**: Kentish men camped at Blackheath. King Richard II went to meet them but retreated to the Tower.
>
> **13 June**: Tyler and Lollard John Ball spoke to the rebels.
>
> **14 June**: Mob stormed into London – attacked Savoy Palace, home of Richard II's uncle, John of Gaunt. The King met Tyler at Mile End and announced the abolition of wage-fixing by Parliament, and an amnesty for all rebels. Tyler demanded the punishment of the King's advisers, but he rejected this. The Essex men killed Archbishop Sudbury.
>
> **15 June**: After a night's rioting in London, Richard and Tyler met again, at Smithfield. Richard bravely faced the rebels, asked them to accept him as their leader, reminded them of his promises and invited them to go home. They did so, and the Revolt was over. The King then punished the rebels' leaders. Tyler was dragged from St Bartholomew's Hospital, beheaded and his head placed on London Bridge, where rebels had put Sudbury's head some days before. Armed forces were sent to arrest other leaders in Kent and Essex and to crush any local risings.
>
> **2 July**: Richard cancelled all his promises to Tyler and the rebels. All of the leaders were killed.

Look back to topic 1.5 to remind yourself who the Lollards were.

The events of 1381 show you that life in the Middle Ages was not as stable as people sometimes think.

However, the **attempt to control wages of the workers did not work**, and increasingly people broke away from their feudal obedience to the landlords, with towns and the new crafts giving them new opportunities. Therefore, the Peasants' Revolt marked a **turning point in history**.

Key Point

- The Revolt was crushed, and the young King Richard II was clever and ruthless.

Fig. 1.36 Richard II at Blackheath, approaching the rebels in his royal barge.

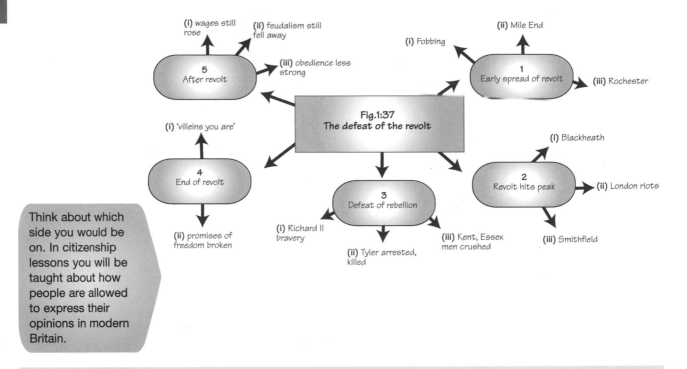

Think about which side you would be on. In citizenship lessons you will be taught about how people are allowed to express their opinions in modern Britain.

Progress Check

1 Name two leaders of the peasants.
2 Who was the King of England in 1381?
3 What tax started off the Peasants' Revolt?
4 Against which country was England fighting before the Revolt?
5 What had Parliament tried to do about peasants' feudal duties?
6 What had Parliament tried to do to wages?
7 What was happening to the self-confidence of people in the 14th century?

7. It was increasing.
1. Wat Tyler, John Ball. 2. Richard II. 3. The poll tax. 4. France. 5. Enforce them. 6. Stop them rising.

1.8 Why were the English able to conquer Wales but not Scotland?

After studying this topic you should be able to:

- understand how Wales was conquered by King Edward I's armies
- appreciate the reasons why the English wanted to expand their power
- understand why Scotland was harder for England to conquer than Wales
- describe how the Welsh and the Scots fought the English
- understand the effects of the English wars on Wales and Scotland.

Edward I and the conquest of Wales

Marches were fortified areas with a castle dominating the countryside.

William I (see topic 1.1) created three powerful **Lords of the Marches** – at Chester, Shrewsbury and Hereford – to prevent any invasions from Wales, where kings of Wales ruled over a number of provinces such as Powys.

The Norman lords built castles and ruled these border areas, with knights farming much of the land, as was normal in the feudal system.

Danger from Welsh archers was common, as is shown by the following eyewitness account from 1188:

> *Two Normans were crossing a bridge to get to safety in a tower built on a mound of earth. The Welsh chased them. Their arrows pierced the thick oaken door of the tower.* (Gerald of Wales)

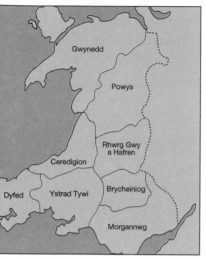

g. 1.38 The provinces of Wales
the time of William I.

During the 13th century the **Welsh fought back**. **Llewelyn 'the great' of Gwynedd** gained control of most of Wales from the English kings, so that in 1216 all Wales accepted his rule.

However, **Edward I** invaded Wales (1276–7) and defeated the Welsh. When they rebelled, he led a second invasion (1282–3) during which Llewelyn was killed. To ensure his control over Wales, Edward built eight great coastal castles. A thousand men worked on the building of another for many years (Harlech) while Beaumaris is described as 'a masterpiece of medieval fortification'.

This eyewitness writer described the Welsh fighters:

> *They are very fierce at the start. But if the enemy resist and they have to retreat, they become confused. They run away and do not try to fight back. Their only tactics are either to chase an enemy or to run away: they do not fight long battles or in hand-to-hand conflict. They harass enemies by ambushes and night attacks.* (Gerald of Wales)

Edward I divided Wales. He made three northern counties (Anglesey, Caernarfon and Merioneth) and two southern ones (Cardigan and Carmarthen). The rest of Wales was ruled by Norman barons. English bishops were put in charge of the Church, and Welsh law was replaced with English law.

King Edward I was a very determined and ruthless king.

The legend of King Arthur and the Knights of the Round Table

The English thought that the Welsh were 'Celtic barbarians'. It is true that they were economically backward, living much as the Saxons had lived in England in the 8th century. In 1139 a Welsh writer, Geoffrey of Monmouth, described a Romano-Celtic 'King' Arthur, who was descended from Aeneas, the mythical founder of Rome. King Arthur's court at Camelot was known for its learning, chivalry and high living.

The failed attempt to conquer Scotland

On Alexander's death (1286) thirteen Scots claimed the throne, leading to a **civil war** in Scotland. At the end of the war, the Scottish leaders met with King Edward I to choose **John Balliol** (1292–6) as King of Scotland – he promised to take the **English King Edward as overlord**.

Fig. 1.39 William Wallace rejects the English proposals at Cambuskenneth.

However, when Balliol refused to supply men and money for Edward's French wars, the English invaded Scotland, defeated Balliol and took the **Coronation Stone from Scone to Westminster in London**. English officials were left in charge of Scotland.

William Wallace, a leading Scottish lord, then led a **guerrilla war against the English**. In 1297 he captured the English headquarters at Stirling and drove the conquerors out of Scotland. In 1298 Edward sent fresh armies which defeated Wallace at Falkirk. Wallace went into hiding, was betrayed by a fellow Scot and was executed.

The execution of William Wallace in 1305 is described by a Norman writer as follows:

> *Wallace … was drawn through London's streets at the tails of horses to an unusually high gallows. There he was hung. He was taken down while still alive: … his bowels torn out, his head cut off, his body divided into four …* (Chronicle of Lanercost, 1320)

However, the execution of Wallace did not crush the desire of Scotland's leaders to be free. In 1306 **Robert Bruce**, one of the claimants to the throne in 1286, had himself crowned at Scone and declared war on England. Defeated at Perth, he fled to Rathlin, off the Irish coast.

The legend is that Bruce was hiding in a cave and saw a spider trying to climb the wall of the cave. Eventually it succeeded. Bruce is supposed to have taken the motto after this: 'If at first you don't succeed, try, try and try again'.

When Edward II became King of England (1307), Bruce returned to Scotland, where he received support from many Scottish people and **formed an army** to defeat the English. Edward II sent 20,000 soldiers.

 Key Points
- The Scottish people were very persistent in resisting English attempts at conquest.
- Wallace and Bruce were key leaders of Scottish resistance.

When you have to remember key dates, draw up a simple time line and place the key events and key people alongside the dates.

Although Bruce had only 7000 men, he won the **Battle of Bannockburn**, which ended the English attempt to take over Scotland for many years.

The Battle of Bannockburn, 1314, was described by an English writer in 1320.

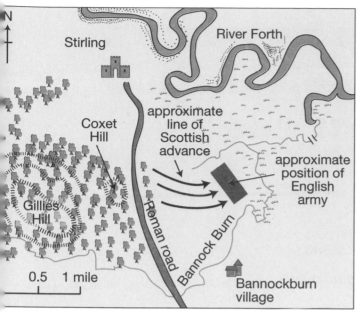

Fig. 1.40 A plan of the Battle of Bannockburn.

As the two armies drew closer, the Scots knelt to say the Lord's prayer before they advanced. They … [were] led by Robert Bruce. The great English horses charged the pikes of the Scots and there was the great noise of broken spears and fatally wounded horses. … Some escaped with great difficulty. Many never got out at all. … I got the account from a trustworthy person who was there. (Chronicle of Lanercost)

After more years of fighting, the English finally signed the Treaty of Northampton (1328) in which Bruce was recognised as King of an independent Scotland. The English realised that they had failed to do to Scotland what they had done to Wales.

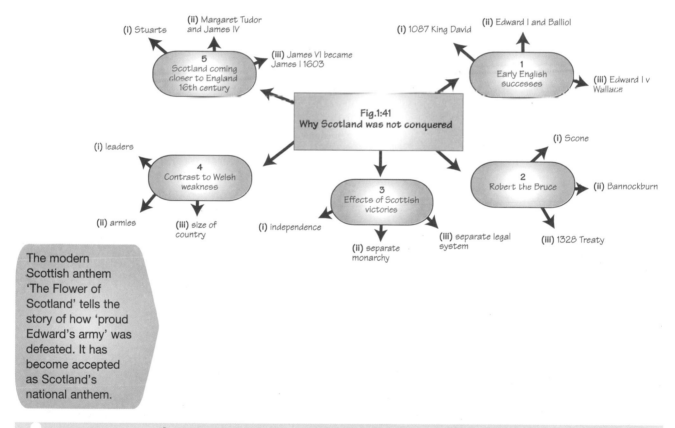

The modern Scottish anthem 'The Flower of Scotland' tells the story of how 'proud Edward's army' was defeated. It has become accepted as Scotland's national anthem.

Progress Check

1 Who led the rebellion against English rule in Wales in the 1270s?
2 What did the English build on the Welsh borders?
3 Which legend was written about the Celts?
4 Where did the Scots finally defeat the English in 1322?
5 Which Scottish king refused to send money and men to Edward?
6 Which Scottish rebel leader was executed by the English?
7 Name the Scottish leader who finally defeated the English.

1. Llewelyn. 2. Castles. 3. The legend of King Arthur and the Knights of the Round Table. 4. Bannockburn. 5. Balliol. 6. Wallace. 7. Bruce.

1.9 How was the monarch's power gradually limited by Parliament and nobles?

After studying this topic you should be able to:

- understand about the Norman Great Council
- know about the Magna Carta
- describe Simon de Montfort's ideas
- understand Edward I's use of Parliament
- describe the fall of Richard II due to his failure to deal with Parliament
- understand the rise of 'new men' and Parliament.

The power of the barons

This topic will show you that during the Middle Ages the monarchs discovered that they could not rule the country like dictators. They needed the support of the leading people.

The Norman kings were not able to rule the country on their own, so they often called a **Great Council** to discuss problems facing the kingdom.

The loss of most of the English lands in France meant that the barons lost a lot of prestige and money. The bishops, who were also powerful landlords, were angry that John (known as 'Bad King John') was stealing church property.

Things got so bad that the barons took over London and would not let King John go into the capital city. The barons and bishops told King John to meet them at Runnymede, near Staines on the bank of the River Thames, for a conference.

Key Point

Magna Carta was a key feudal document which showed that the King's power was limited. The King needed the support of his nobles.

King John was forced to sign the famous **Magna Carta** (Great Charter) in which he agreed to **respect the rights of the landlords**. The charter had 63 clauses. The King was limited in how much tax he could charge, and had to promise not to imprison a man without a fair trial.

The Charter was updated in 1225 and it showed that the powers of the King were becoming more limited. John died trying to escape from the barons in 1216, so he did not learn the lessons of Magna Carta.

Parliament becomes more powerful

> In Britain we now have elections to form our government every five years.

Henry III (1216–72) was only nine when he became king, so his brother-in-law, Simon de Montfort, ruled instead of him until Henry was 16. In 1258 de Montfort led a **rebellion** by the barons against Henry's high taxes.

de Montfort organised the **election** of two **knights** from each county, and two **rich men** from each chartered town. They met at Westminster Abbey, so de Montfort is really the man who began the British Parliament and general elections.

King Edward I (1272–1307) went along with these ideas, because he accepted that he needed 'the consent of all the realm'. In 1295 he called the '**model Parliament**' – the representatives of the counties and the towns met in Westminster to discuss the running of the country. Edward I, therefore, is the co-founder of Parliament along with de Montfort.

Edward called people to Parliament because he needed the barons, knights and townspeople to agree to pay taxes so that he could fight the Welsh, the Scots and the French in a long series of wars.

> **Key Point**
>
> Taxation was the key reason for the rise of Parliament. The King needed MPs to vote for the taxes so that he could take money from the people of the country.

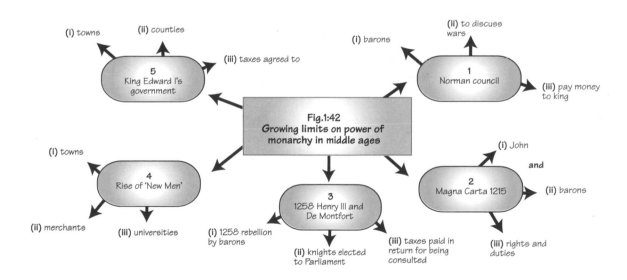

Fig.1:42
Growing limits on power of monarchy in middle ages

1 Norman council
(i) barons
(ii) to discuss wars
(iii) pay money to king

2 Magna Carta 1215
(i) John and
(ii) barons
(iii) rights and duties

3 1258 Henry III and De Montfort
(i) 1258 rebellion by barons
(ii) knights elected to Parliament
(iii) taxes paid in return for being consulted

4 Rise of 'New Men'
(i) towns
(ii) merchants
(iii) universities

5 King Edward I's government
(i) towns
(ii) counties
(iii) taxes agreed to

King Richard II (1367–99) was not as sensible as Edward I. He believed that there should be 'no earthly subjugation in anything touching the crown'. Richard's attempts to run the country **without the consent of the leading people** from the counties and the towns caused the **barons to overthrow** him and replace him with **Henry Bolingbroke**.

By 1500, **Parliament** was a very **important part** of the running of the country.

The limited power of the King

Fig. 1.43 The Houses of Parliament.

By 1500, as a result of a series of upheavals, the **King's power** was much more **limited** than it was in 1066.

- People no longer thought that the King's power could not be questioned.
- The court system had been developed and jury trials were common.
- Parliament had to give consent for any new or increased taxes.
- The big towns like London and Norwich were difficult to control and the townspeople had great pride in their town's independence.

However, the King still had many powers.

- The King could call Parliament and send MPs home.
- He could win friends by giving people jobs and giving people places in court.
- An effective king like Henry II, Edward I or Henry VII was still able to run the country.
- A king who was good at dealing with people tactfully and firmly was still very powerful.

The growing importance of Parliament

Parliament grew in importance under the **Tudors** from 1485–1603, building on what had gone before in the 14th and 15th centuries.

Henry VIII (1509–47) had to call for money for his wars against France and Scotland. He used Parliament to pass the laws he needed to make his break with Rome legal.

Most Parliaments did what monarchs wanted. Henry VIII got his reformation; Edward VI's Parliaments passed anti-Catholic laws; Mary got her Catholic laws through. Elizabeth I (1558–1603) called many Parliaments. It was during this reign that MPs first challenged the sovereign's rights, and so prepared the way for the more serious disputes with the Stuart Kings James I, Charles I and James II.

Progress Check

1 Who were the two founders of Parliament?
2 What did the barons make King John sign in 1215?
3 Where were the members of Parliament from?
4 Name the king removed in 1399.
5 Why did kings need money during the Middle Ages?
6 Which royal dynasty went on to make Parliament even more powerful?

1. Simon De Montfort and King Edward I. 2. The Magna Carta. 3. Towns and counties. 4. Richard II. 5. To pay for wars in France. 6. The Tudors.

The following practice questions focus on 'changes and situations' in the knowledge and understanding strand of the History National Curriculum.

1   Study the text and all the sources in topic 1.1 on why William of Normandy conquered England in 1066 and answer the following question.

   Write a bullet point list of the claims to the English throne made by the English King Harold, Harald Hardrada of Norway and William, Duke of Normandy.   **[10]**

2   Write a series of paragraphs explaining how the new King William I made sure that England was going to be kept under his control after he won the Battle of Hastings. Use the following points as your paragraph headings: **[25]**

   • The feudal system – [*The feudal system helped William to control England because…*]
   • The building of castles – [*Castles were an effective method of control because…*]
   • The Oath of Salisbury – [*The Oath of Salisbury made William's control greater because…*]
   • Crushing of rebellions – [*William ruthlessly crushed rebels to show that…*]
   • The writing of the Domesday Book – [*This famous book reinforced the message that William was in charge and the country belonged to him because…*]

3   On an A3 sheet of paper, draw four columns. Label the columns as follows: **[20]**

   • Reasons for building castles
   • Methods of defending castles
   • Methods of attacking castles
   • Developments in castle building.
   Make a list of bullet points in the appropriate columns.
   Colour code your answers: one colour for each column.

4   a Write an account of the stages by which a young man prepared to become a knight.   **[5]**
   b Do you think the life and duties of a knight were easy?
      Give reasons for your answer.   **[5]**
   c What were the main reasons why people became knights in the Middle Ages?   **[5]**

5   Do you agree that life in the medieval village was very hard for villagers? Give detailed reasons for your answers. Refer to the following aspects of medieval life: **[18]**

   • the villagers' use of the manor fields
   • types of work on the land
   • the Black Death.

6 Draw a spidergram in which you summarise the following aspects of the impact of religion in England: **[10]**

- bishops
- monasteries
- cathedrals
- priests
- daily Church life
- Lollards.

You could draw each aspect in a different colour.

7 What changes did people experience as English towns developed during the Middle Ages? Refer in your answer to the lives of the following key groups of people in the towns: **[10]**

- craftsmen
- wool merchants
- shop-keepers
- exporters.

8 Explain how the anger of the following groups of people led to the Peasants' Revolt in 1381. **[20]**

- **Peasants** *Peasants were driven to revolt by...*
- **Ex-soldiers** *Ex-soldiers added to the wave of protest by...*
- **Religious protesters** *Religion was another cause of protest because...*
- **Tax-payers** *Tax-payers became more and more angry with the government because...*
- **Leaders like Ball and Tyler** *Wat Tyler and John Ball were important leaders of the people because...*

9 Make a list of the differences and the similarities between events in Wales and Scotland when the English attempted to conquer those nations. **[10]**

10 Write three paragraphs on how the power of the monarch was gradually limited using the following headings: **[15]**

- The barons' actions over the writing of Magna Carta
- Simon de Montfort's leadership
- King Edward I's own actions.

2 British history 1500–1750

2.1 How much did Henry VIII and his son Edward VI change the Church in England?

After studying this topic you should understand:

- why Henry VIII led the Church in England to break away from the Catholic Church
- why many people supported Henry VIII's new religious policies
- why many people opposed these policies
- how the Church in England was affected over the period 1509–53
- how Edward VI's reign was different from Henry VIII's reign.

> The term 'Reformation' refers to the fact that a new Church – the Protestant Church – was formed in England.

Although when Henry VIII became King in 1509 he was a **Catholic**, by the end of his reign in 1547, England's Church had broken away from the Catholic Church. This dramatic event started the **English Reformation**.

In 1520 Martin Luther, a German monk, attacked many Catholic beliefs, such as the **mass** and the **power of the Pope**. His followers were known as **Protestants** because they were protesting against the Catholic Church.

Henry VIII was awarded the title 'Defender of the Faith' by the **Pope** for a book which he wrote attacking Luther's ideas.

Henry VIII's attempts to father a son

Henry wanted above all to have a healthy son, so that the **Tudor family** could continue in power and **civil war would be avoided**. His father, Henry VII, arranged for him to marry **Catherine of Aragon**, widow of his brother Prince Arthur, and Henry had a daughter, **Mary**, but not the son he wanted.

Henry VIII then fell in love with **Anne Boleyn**, so in 1527 he sent his Archbishop of Canterbury, Cardinal Wolsey, to ask the Pope to let him divorce Catherine. But the Pope refused Henry's request because remarriage was forbidden by the Bible. Henry was angry. He removed Wolsey from office and appointed Thomas Cranmer as his Archbishop.

Cranmer declared that Henry was never really married to Catherine, so Henry **divorced** Catherine and married Anne Boleyn in June 1533. She gave birth to a girl three months later. Her name was **Elizabeth**.

As is well known, Henry went on to marry four more wives after Anne Boleyn (see the family tree below). Thomas Cranmer loyally helped King Henry VIII get rid of his wives on five occasions, including having two of them executed!

Key Point — **Henry's marriage problem, his 'Great Matter', was the key reason for the English Reformation.**

Henry becomes head of the Church in England

The Pope **excommunicated Henry** and his supporters, so in 1534 Parliament named Henry the **Supreme Head of the Church**, and everyone had to sign an oath to say that they accepted this new law.

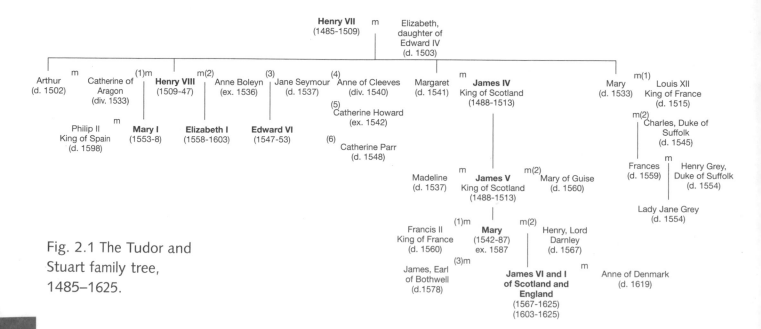

Fig. 2.1 The Tudor and Stuart family tree, 1485–1625.

Remember that religion was very important to people. In the 16th century Catholics believed that a person who was excommunicated (thrown out of the Church) would go to hell.

Most bishops and priests in England accepted this. Loyal Catholics who refused to accept this law or to sign an oath that Anne Boleyn was the true wife of the King were executed.

Thomas More (the Chancellor of England), John Fisher (the Bishop of Rochester) and the Glastonbury monks were all executed for treason because they would not accept that the King was head of the Church. Catholics praise them as martyrs.

The closure of the monasteries

Henry then **closed all the monasteries** (1537–9) and took all their land. The sale of this land gave him an income of £100,000 a year for some years, double his usual income. The land was bought cheaply by MPs, courtiers and other influential people, who were then anxious to maintain the break with Rome. The monastic buildings fell into disrepair.

The monasteries (see topic 1.5) had been important centres of education and help for the poor and the sick, so their closure affected England very much. The man who organised the closures was **Thomas Cromwell**, who sent a group of inspectors to the monasteries to prove that the monks and nuns were greedy and badly behaved.

Executing both Catholics and Protestants

Fig. 2.2 Executing rebels who took part in the Pilgrimage of Grace.

Many people were angry with the changes. A nobleman called **Robert Aske** led the **Pilgrimage of Grace** in 1536 to protest, but Henry ordered the execution of Aske and his followers. Several **monks were executed** on the hill at **Glastonbury** and their bodies were left to hang in the wind for weeks, as a warning to people to abandon the old Catholic faith.

However, Henry was not opposed to the main Catholic teachings, about the mass, the Virgin Mary, confession and the celibacy (non-marriage) of priests (all of which Lutherans opposed). Henry VIII passed a law in 1539 to outlaw the teachings of Lutherans, and his government still burned Protestants.

Protestants were people who were protesting against the Catholic Church. They objected to the power of the Pope and the priests. They disliked Catholic practices like the mass, praying for the dead, praying to saints and praying to the Virgin Mary.

Fig. 2.3 Burning Lutherans.

By the time Henry VIII died in 1547, he had allowed his son, the future King Edward VI, to be educated by Protestants, and Thomas Cranmer was busy rewriting the words of Church services to please the growing number of Protestants who had been coming to England from Germany and Switzerland.

The Reformation under Edward VI

Edward VI's government changed the Church very quickly. Edward became King at the age of nine, so the religious changes were pushed through by **Thomas Cranmer** and the **leading nobles** (the **Council**).

Key Point The Reformation process speeded up under Edward VI's government.

If you go on holiday to a Catholic country like Italy, France or Spain, you could go into a Catholic church and see what churches looked like in England before the Reformation.

Chantries were closed down in 1547. These were small chapels where masses were said for the dead.

The most important change was the **new Protestant Prayer Book** (1549 and 1552 versions). The prayer book replaced the mass. It put forward the belief that the bread and wine used in the service remained only bread and wine. Stone altars were replaced by **wooden tables**. Vestments were **simplified**. Statues and stained glass windows were smashed up, because Protestants considered them to be idols. Protestants believed in basing their faith on the Bible and that the Catholic Church had moved away from true religion.

Catholic protesters, like the people of Exeter who in 1549 asked for the return of the mass and the old images of the Catholic faith, were hanged.

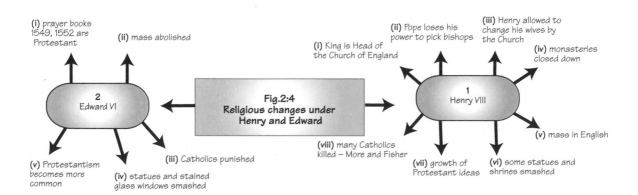

(i) prayer books 1549, 1552 are Protestant

(ii) mass abolished

(ii) Pope loses his power to pick bishops

(iii) Henry allowed to change his wives by the Church

(i) King is Head of the Church of England

(iv) monasteries closed down

2 Edward VI

Fig.2:4 Religious changes under Henry and Edward

1 Henry VIII

(v) mass in English

(v) Protestantism becomes more common

(iii) Catholics punished

(iv) statues and stained glass windows smashed

(viii) many Catholics killed – More and Fisher

(vii) growth of Protestant ideas

(vi) some statues and shrines smashed

Edward VI even stopped his sister Mary Tudor going to mass, as the following quotation from her shows:

> *My duty most humbly remembered unto your Majesty ... I trusted that you would have allowed me your poor sister to have the traditional mass, which the King, your father and mine, with all his predecessors had.* (Letter from Princess Mary, 1547)

By 1553, when Edward died at the age of 15, England had become a **truly Protestant country**.

Progress Check

1 Whose writings did Henry VIII attack?
2 What title did the Pope give Henry VIII?
3 Who did Henry VIII wish to marry by 1530?
4 Name the Archbishop who replaced Wolsey.
5 Why was More executed?
6 Who led the 'Pilgrimage of Grace'?
7 Which king's government pushed through many changes in religion?

1. Martin Luther. 2. Defender of the Faith. 3. Anne Boleyn. 4. Thomas Cranmer. 5. Because he opposed Henry VIII's laws. 6. Robert Aske. 7. Edward VI.

2.2 Was Queen Mary Tudor (1553–1558) really 'Bloody Mary'?

After studying this topic you should be able to:

- **explain why Mary ordered the burning of so many Protestants**
- **explain why she was hated by Protestants**
- **explain the effects of her policies on the English Church**
- **compare her policies to the other Tudor monarchs**
- **evaluate whether she was a successful ruler.**

A return to Catholicism

Fig. 2.5 Mary Tudor.

When Mary became queen at the age of 37, she was determined to make England a Catholic country again. Many leading Protestant preachers and writers fled to Germany and Switzerland.

Queen Mary married the strongly Catholic **King Philip II of Spain**. Many people in England were angry about this because they feared that if Mary had a child, the Spanish throne would have power over England. The Spanish King behaved in a very cruel way towards Protestants in Spain and people feared that his methods would spread to England.

These victims of Mary Tudor are hailed as martyrs by members of Protestant Churches.

Mary ordered 284 Protestants to be burned to death because of their faith, as a way of frightening people into obeying her Catholic laws.

Mary compelled people to **attend mass** again, to accept the new **statues**, **stone altars** and prayers to the **Virgin Mary**. She also forced people to accept the **authority of the Pope** over religion in England.

Mary's burnings of Protestants shocked many people. The following famous excerpt from John Foxe's *Book of Martyrs* describes how the Lutherans **Latimer** and **Ridley** were burned in the centre of Oxford in 1555. Foxe wrote his book to encourage people to reject the Catholic religion and to become committed Protestants.

> *So they came to the stake. Dr Ridley, entering the place first, looked towards Heaven. Then, seeing Mr Latimer, with a cheerful look, he ran and embraced him saying, 'Be of good heart, brother, for God will either ease the fury of the flame, or else strengthen us to endure it.'*
>
> *Dr Ridley's brother brought him a bag of gunpowder and tied it about his neck. Then they brought a lighted faggot and laid it at Dr Ridley's feet. Mr Latimer said: 'Be of good comfort, Dr Ridley, we shall this day light such a candle, by God's grace, in England, as I trust never shall be put out.' He then cried out, 'Father of Heaven, receive my soul.'*
>
> (John Foxe's *Book of Martyrs*, 1583)

Key Point

Mary was trying to reverse 20 years of religious change.

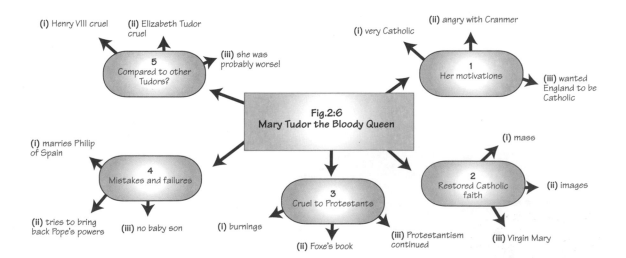

Fig.2:6
Mary Tudor the Bloody Queen

5 Compared to other Tudors?
(i) Henry VIII cruel
(ii) Elizabeth Tudor cruel
(iii) she was probably worse!

1 Her motivations
(i) very Catholic
(ii) angry with Cranmer
(iii) wanted England to be Catholic

4 Mistakes and failures
(i) marries Philip of Spain
(ii) tries to bring back Pope's powers
(iii) no baby son

3 Cruel to Protestants
(i) burnings
(ii) Foxe's book
(iii) Protestantism continued

2 Restored Catholic faith
(i) mass
(ii) images
(iii) Virgin Mary

Foxe's writings have become very famous and most history books do not describe the killing of Catholics. History is often written by the winners.

The courage of the people who were executed also persuaded people to become Protestants, especially in London and Kent. Mary seemed particularly cruel, and gave the Catholic faith a bad reputation.

The map below shows the places where Protestants were burned. You will notice that most burnings took place in southern England.

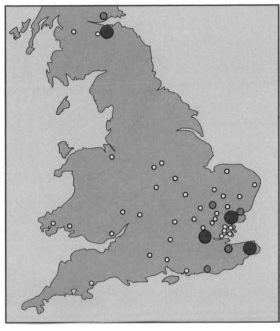

Number of burnings:
○ under 3
● 20
● 74

Fig. 2.7 The locations of the burning of Protestants.

A cruel age

When we look at the way the other Tudor monarchs behaved, we can see that although she was a cruel ruler, the other monarchs were also cruel. More than 80 people were burned under Henry VIII. Two were burned under Edward VI, and five under Elizabeth I.

However, these monarchs also ordered many to be hanged, drawn and quartered for going to the Catholic mass and trying to convert people back to Catholicism. It can be argued that **Queen Mary deserves the title 'Bloody Mary'** and that the **other Tudors were also 'bloody'**. The **Tudor age** was a **cruel period of English history**.

Mary's successor

Mary's reign ended after only five years in 1588. She suffered from ill health and she was disappointed when she failed to have a baby, so that England could remain Catholic.

Progress Check

1 In which year did Mary become queen, after Edward died?
2 Whom did she marry?
3 Name two famous Protestant martyrs.
4 What changes did Mary make to the Church in England?
5 What were the effects of the burnings of Protestants?
6 Who succeeded Mary as queen in 1558?

1. 1553. 2. Philip of Spain. 3. Latimer and Ridley. 4. She brought back the mass, statues, stone altars, prayers to Virgin Mary, authority of Pope. 5. They encouraged Protestants. 6. Elizabeth Tudor.

2.3 How successful was Elizabeth Tudor (1558–1603) in solving the 'religious problem'?

After studying this topic you should be able to:

- describe how Elizabeth Tudor (Elizabeth I) tried to avoid a religious war in England
- understand how Elizabeth attempted to bring the English people together under one religion
- understand Catholic attitudes towards Elizabeth's policies
- understand Puritan attitudes towards these policies
- evaluate whether Elizabeth's policies were successful.

A single Anglican Church

Elizabeth's main aim was to **unite the people** of the country in one **Anglican Church**, with as wide an appeal as possible. Her policy was called at the time *via media* – a **middle way** between the ideas of devout Catholics and devout Protestants.

> **Key Point**
>
> Elizabeth I is often regarded as the country's greatest monarch. She became queen at the age of 25; a young woman in a very male world. England had never been ruled by an unmarried woman before. When she took the the throne, many people thought she would not survive as ruler.

Elizabeth aimed to please as many people as possible by allowing them to believe in a wide set of ideas, provided they obeyed the law and lived peacefully. In 1559 she worked with Parliament to produce the famous laws of her '**religious settlement**'.

- Everyone was **obliged to attend** their local parish church on Sunday, with non-attendance punished by a fine followed by imprisonment. Services were in **English** (Catholic services had been in Latin) and **vicars could marry**.

- In the new Prayer Book, the words of Cranmer's Communion Service combined the words of the older 1547 and the 1552 prayer books to allow people to believe either the Catholic teaching about **Holy Communion**, or the new Protestant teaching.

- The service was in **English** instead of Latin, so that ordinary people, not just priests and well-off educated people, could read and understand the words. This pleased Protestants.

Remember the Catholic teaching was that the bread and wine was transformed into the body of Jesus Christ during the service, while the Protestant belief was that it remained bread and wine, and the ritual was merely symbolic.

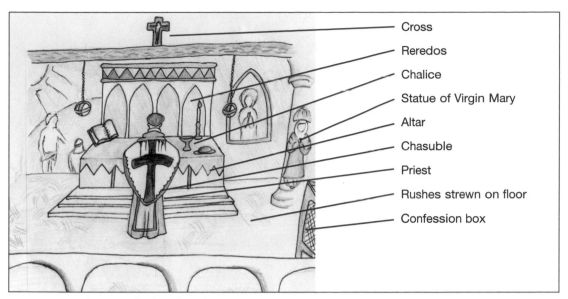

Cross

Reredos

Chalice

Statue of Virgin Mary

Altar

Chasuble

Priest

Rushes strewn on floor

Confession box

Fig. 2.8 Inside a Catholic church.

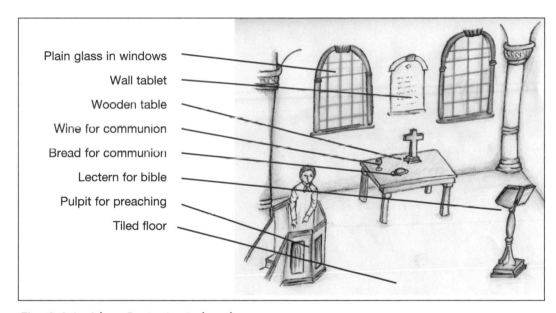

Plain glass in windows

Wall tablet

Wooden table

Wine for communion

Bread for communion

Lectern for bible

Pulpit for preaching

Tiled floor

Fig. 2.9 Inside a Protestant church.

- **Simple vestments** (clothes) and **candles** still had to be used in church to give ceremonies a sense of mystery. This pleased most Catholics and most Protestants, but annoyed some of both faiths.

- **The Pope had no power** over the English Church and Elizabeth appointed all the bishops who all vowed that they accepted the Protestant religion. This pleased all the Protestants and annoyed many Catholics.

- To avoid annoying Catholics and Puritans, Elizabeth called herself the **'Supreme Governor'** of the Church, instead of the old title, 'Supreme Head'.

- Gradually under Elizabeth almost all the **statues, stained glass windows** and **crucifixes** were removed from the churches. This pleased the

> Remember that religious laws had a huge impact on people, since they all went to church at least once a week, and the Church was at the centre of people's lives.

Protestants, who did not like religious images, which they believed were condemned in the Bible.

- **Praying for the dead** was banned, because the new Prayer Book said that people went to heaven if they had faith.
- **Sermons** had to be given by the vicar every week to persuade them to be loyal to the new Church of England. This is a good example of religion being used as a form of **propaganda**.

 Key Point

Elizabeth I was a very clever ruler, as was shown by her religious laws.

The persecution of Catholics

Most Catholics were satisfied but a **minority** wanted a full return to the authority of **Rome**. One Catholic priest, Edmund Campion, for example, was tortured and executed on false charges.

Some **loyal Catholics**, such as Lord Howard, who commanded the English fleet against the Spanish Armada (see topic 2.5), were allowed to continue as **Catholics in private**. But poorer people could not afford the fines for not attending church.

> Loyal Catholics were called 'Papists' because of their loyalty to the Pope. The word Pope comes from the Latin word for father.

Francis Walsingham was given the job of hunting down Catholic priests and Catholics who attended mass in their own homes. Priests often hid in **'priest holes'** in big houses owned by Catholic nobles, but they were often caught when neighbours betrayed them.

In some areas of the country, especially northern England many people stayed loyal to their old faith.

Puritan resistance

> The term 'Puritan' was originally an insult said by people who were either still Catholic or were happy with Elizabeth's Anglican Church.

Most Protestants were pleased with the changes made by Elizabeth, but the more enthusiastic Protestants known as **Puritans** were angry. They were called Puritans because they wanted a purer religion with nothing left from Catholicism. They wanted a religion based purely on what was in the Bible.

Some Puritans went to Anglican churches and persuaded vicars to simplify the services more than the Prayer Book had done. However, extreme Puritans refused to go to church and **met in their own homes**.

Elizabeth had many extreme Puritans **arrested**. John Stubbs had his hand cut off for criticising the Queen in a book. Puritans were considered more dangerous than Catholics.

Certain aspects of Church teachings and customs continued unchanged through the Reformation, such as the importance of the church building, the minister, prayer and rites of passage at times of birth, marriage and death.

The following quotation from a writer at the time explains the Puritans' beliefs:

There is a sect in England called Puritans. These, following Calvin's teachings, reject all ancient ceremonies, they do not allow any organs or altars in their places of worship. They oppose any differences in rank among churchmen, such as bishops, deans, etc. (P. Hentzner, 1598)

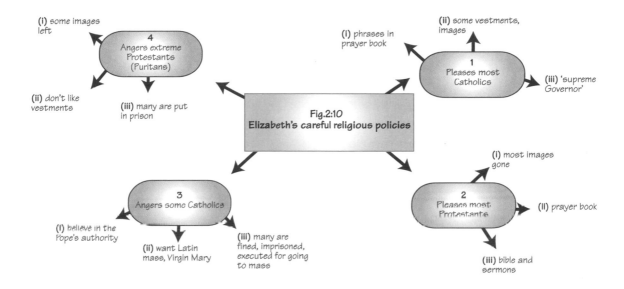

Fig.2:10
Elizabeth's careful religious policies

4 Angers extreme Protestants (Puritans)
(i) some images left
(ii) don't like vestments
(iii) many are put in prison

1 Pleases most Catholics
(i) phrases in prayer book
(ii) some vestments, images
(iii) 'supreme Governor'

3 Angers some Catholics
(i) believe in the Pope's authority
(ii) want Latin mass, Virgin Mary
(iii) many are fined, imprisoned, executed for going to mass

2 Pleases most Protestants
(i) most images gone
(ii) prayer book
(iii) bible and sermons

By 1603, when Elizabeth died, the generations of people who could remember Catholic England had also died, so England had become a **Protestant country** in a fairly peaceful manner.

Progress Check

1 What name have historians given to Elizabeth I's religious policy?
2 Name two groups of people who did not like her religious policy.
3 Who was in charge of hunting down the rebellious Catholics?
4 What happened to people if they did not go to church?
5 In what part of England did Catholics remain numerous?
6 What did extreme Puritans do?

1. The via media. 2. Puritans and Catholics. 3. Francis Walsingham. 4. They were fined then imprisoned if they carried on breaking the law. 5. Northern England. 6. Met in their own houses instead of going to church.

2.4 Why was Mary Queen of Scots a problem for Queen Elizabeth I and how did Elizabeth respond to the threat?

After studying this topic you should be able to:

● **explain how Mary Queen of Scots was related to Elizabeth I**
● **show why Mary was a threat to Elizabeth**
● **understand how this threat grew over time**
● **understand the alternatives Elizabeth had in her dealings with Mary**
● **assess the reasons why Mary was executed.**

Mary Queen of Scots was **Elizabeth's Catholic cousin**, as the family tree on page 44 shows.

The threat from Mary

Mary Queen of Scots, sometimes called Mary Stuart, was a **threat to Queen Elizabeth** for many reasons.

Don't get Mary Queen of Scots mixed up with 'Bloody Mary'. Elizabeth was sister of 'Bloody Mary' and succeeded her as queen of England. Mary Queen of Scots was Elizabeth's cousin.

● Mary believed she had a **claim to the English throne** because she was related to King Henry VIII.

● Therefore there was a rival royal princess in England with potential **Catholic support**, especially in northern England. Elizabeth had ordered the execution of hundreds of Catholic northern rebels.

● Many **English Protestants were worried** that Mary Queen of Scots would become **Queen** in England after Elizabeth died because Elizabeth had not married and there were no Tudors left. This revived memories of all the trouble with the burnings of Protestants by 'Bloody Mary' (see topic 2.2).

● Elizabeth and her advisors feared that Mary Stuart would **ally with France and Spain**. Their Catholic kings could then invade England, remove the Protestant religion, restore Catholicism and take all the lands of the Protestant families.

● Mary was also accused of the **murder** of her second husband, **Lord Darnley**, so she was regarded as even more dangerous.

Key Point

The threat from Mary Queen of Scots shows how dangerous a time it was for Queen Elizabeth.

Elizabeth's dilemma

Fig. 2.11 Elizabeth 1.

Some of Elizabeth's advisors said that she should order Mary to be executed, but **Elizabeth was cautious** about this. Mary was, after all, her cousin and she did not want to be called a murderer.

So, Elizabeth kept Mary in **prison** for 19 years, but this was not the end of the matter, since fellow Catholics plotted to release her on several occasions. One of the plotters was the Italian nobleman **Ridolfi** who, alongside the leading Catholic the **Duke of Norfolk**, was **executed** in 1572 for **treason**.

In 1586 **Francis Walsingham**, Elizabeth's chief spy, set a trap for Mary and found evidence that **she was plotting to kill Elizabeth**.

At last Walsingham managed to persuade Elizabeth to get rid of Mary and she was put on trial and found **guilty of treason** in October 1586.

For a long time Elizabeth refused to sign the order for Mary to be executed. However, on 8 February 1587 **Mary was executed** at Fotheringay Castle. Mary's famous last words were "Into your hands I commend my spirit". She told her executioner that she wanted to die as a Catholic martyr.

Elizabeth was very **distressed** by the execution. Davison, who had brought the death warrant for her to sign, was sent to the Tower of London. Elizabeth also punished Davison with an enormous fine, which bankrupted him.

What sort of ruler was Elizabeth?

The way Elizabeth I treated her cousin Mary Queen of Scots tells us many things about the sort of queen that Elizabeth had become by 1587.

- Elizabeth was sometimes cautious and found it hard to make up her mind about difficult decisions.
- She was dependent on her senior advisors to make some big decisions.
- She was surrounded by enemies at home, as well as by supporters.
- She always had to think about how Spain and France would react to her actions.
- She seems to have been quite a sensitive person. She was not as ruthless as her father (Henry VIII) or her elder sister (Queen Mary).

Elizabeth's supporters called her the 'Fairy Queen' and paintings were produced to show her as the 'Glorious Queen', with beautiful clothes and in triumphant settings.

Progress Check

1 What was the relationship of Mary Queen of Scots to Queen Elizabeth I?
2 What was Mary's religion?
3 Who trapped Mary into a plot against Elizabeth?
4 Name the two European countries who might have allied with Mary.
5 Who was the secretary who brought Mary's death warrant to Elizabeth?
6 How did Elizabeth react to Mary's execution?
7 When was Mary executed?

6. She was distressed. 7. 8 February 1587.
1. Cousin. 2. Catholic. 3. Francis Walsingham. 4. France and Spain. 5. Davison.

2.5 Why was Philip II of Spain such a problem for Elizabeth and how did Elizabeth deal with the threats from Spain?

After studying this topic you should be able to:

● understand why Philip II of Spain wanted to invade England in 1588
● understand how Philip planned to join his armada with the Spanish armies
● know how the English defenders were able to defeat the armada
● appreciate the part played by Elizabeth in the defeat of the armada
● understand the role of luck in helping the English to defeat the Spanish
● understand how Protestants and Catholics reacted to the armada's defeat.

Why did Philip II want to conquer England?

King Philip II of Spain, the widower of Queen Mary (see topic 2.2), was **the most powerful ruler in Europe** in 1587. He wanted to **conquer England**, to become even more powerful. He believed he had been sent by God to **make England a Catholic country again**, because he was a devout Catholic.

Philip had many reasons to hate England; a combination of **religious and political reasons**.

● **Elizabeth**, to him, was not the lawful queen because she was the **daughter of Anne Boleyn** and Henry VIII (see topic 2.1).

● Elizabeth allowed and rewarded English pirates like Francis Drake when they **raided Spanish ships** and stole Spanish treasure.

● Elizabeth ordered the **torturing of Catholic priests** and the **imprisonment of Catholics** who went to mass (see topic 2.3)

● Elizabeth ordered the **execution** of the Catholic **Mary Queen of Scots** (see topic 2.4), the rightful heir to the throne of England from Philip's point of view.

The Spanish armada

Philip planned to attack England with the famously huge **armada**. He planned to send a **great fleet of ships** from Spain under the top commander Admiral Santa Cruz. This armada was told to sail from Spain to

France in the **crescent formation** and land at Calais, where it would join up with the **Duke of Parma's army**. The crescent formation was hard to attack.

Fig. 2.12 A crescent formation.

From there, the Spanish planned to **invade England** and join up with Catholics who still hated Elizabeth.

Key Point
- The Spanish armada was sent for a combination of reasons and was defeated by a combination of luck, Spanish mistakes and English naval skills.

Elizabeth's commanders ordered **beacons** to be built all **around the coast** of England. These were to be lit when the guards saw the ships coming. When people saw the fires they were to light their own fires.

Why did the Spanish invasion fail?

Fortunately for Elizabeth and England, the Spanish plan broke down for many reasons.

The brilliant **Santa Cruz died** before the armada left, and the new commander, the **Duke of Medina Sidonia**, was **not a good leader**. He suffered from sea-sickness, and was also doubtful whether the plan could work. **Francis Drake**, in a daring attack on the Spanish fleet in Cadiz, damaged many of Philip's ships. Drake said he had *burned the King of Spain's beard*.

When the Spanish finally left Spain in May 1588, the fleet was **damaged by storms**, and **sailors mutinied** due to lack of food and pay. **Lord Howard**, the commander of the English fleet, attacked in the English Channel, so further weakening the Spanish.

When the armada eventually got to **Calais** on 6th August, the Spanish ships did not go into the port because of **storms**, so the English were able to attack them on the open seas, by the clever tactic of **setting fire to old ships** and sending them into the Spanish ships.

The Spanish eventually sailed round England, then Scotland and Ireland and back to Spain.

Victory for England and Elizabeth

Queen Elizabeth went to Tilbury and gave her famous victory speech. Her words made her famous throughout England and Europe:

> *Though I have the body of a feeble woman, I have the heart and stomach of a King, and a King of England too, and think it foul scorn that Parma or Spain or any Prince of Europe should dare to invade the borders of my realm … We shall shortly have a famous victory over these enemies of my God, of my Kingdom, and of my People.*

The English soldiers and leading men of England were very impressed by Elizabeth's speech and the country became more patriotic and confident after the defeat of the most powerful country in Europe. Protestant preachers told the people in church that God had helped England to victory. England was now safe from invasion.

The victory over the Spanish was a turning point in English history and for Elizabeth.

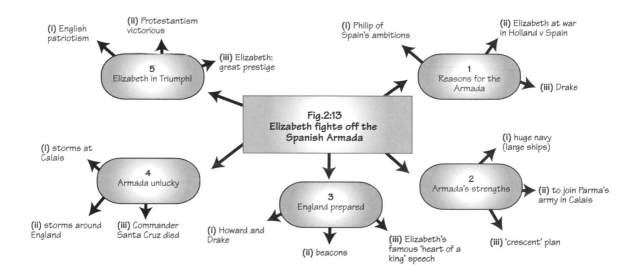

(i) English patriotism

(ii) Protestantism victorious

(iii) Elizabeth: great prestige

5 Elizabeth in Triumph!

(i) Philip of Spain's ambitions

(ii) Elizabeth at war in Holland v Spain

1 Reasons for the Armada

(iii) Drake

Fig.2:13 Elizabeth fights off the Spanish Armada

(i) storms at Calais

4 Armada unlucky

(ii) storms around England

(iii) Commander Santa Cruz died

3 England prepared

(i) Howard and Drake

(ii) beacons

(iii) Elizabeth's famous 'heart of a king' speech

2 Armada's strengths

(i) huge navy (large ships)

(ii) to join Parma's army in Calais

(iii) 'crescent' plan

Progress Check

1 Who was the King of Spain, responsible for the armada?
2 Give three reasons for his attack on England.
3 Where did he plan to join up with the Spanish army?
4 Name two English sailors who led the English defences.
5 What was the effect of the victory on Queen Elizabeth?
6 Who did Protestants in England thank for the victory?

1. Philip II. 2. To make England a Catholic country; because Elizabeth was not legitimate monarch; because England supported Dutch and pirates. 3. Calais. 4. Francis Drake, Lord Howard. 5. She was regarded as a great leader. 6. God.

2.6 What was the impact of Elizabeth's reign on England?

After studying this topic you should be able to:

- understand how Elizabeth made England richer
- explain the role of merchants in making England richer
- understand how merchant companies were formed
- assess the reasons for rising living standards in England under Elizabeth
- appreciate the long-term effects on England of Elizabeth's policies
- compare the lives of the rich merchants with the lives of the poor.

Overseas trade and colonies

Under Queen Elizabeth I **England began to become much richer**, beginning a process of making the country the richest country in the world.

 Key Point

England became very rich due to her development of overseas trade and colonies.

Elizabeth encouraged British merchants and pirates to gain more wealth and power for England to rival such European countries as, for example, Portugal and Spain.

Adventurous sailors such as **Humphrey Gilbert**, **Francis Drake**, **Martin Frobisher** and others faced great dangers as they sailed their small ships, knowing that Spanish and Portuguese fleets might attack them.

The merchant companies

Elizabethans formed **merchant companies** to trade with the wider world. Each company had its **royal charter** giving its members the monopoly of trade in a certain area.

For example, the Muscovy Company (set up in 1553) traded goods with Russia, as can be seen in the following extract:

5th May 1560. The goods we want you to prepare for our ships to carry are wax, tallow, oils, flax, cables and ropes, and furs, mainly sables. We look for a trade worth £3000. (Directors of the Muscovy Company to their agent in Russia, Anthony Jenkinson, 1560)

Key Point

Under Elizabeth England became a great trading nation and began to build an empire. The trade brought wealth into the country and made many people rich.

England became the **most successful trading nation** by 1589, according to this eyewitness:

> The English in searching every quarter of the globe have excelled all the nations. For who before this reign, had ever seen the Caspian Sea, or Constantinople? … What English ships before this anchored in the River Plate, went through the straits of Magellan, travelled the coast of Chile, went to the Philippines in spite of the enemy?   (Richard Hakluyt, 1589)

> In Chapter 6 you will see how the slave trade was abolished in the 19th century.

Merchants from Bristol and Liverpool also developed the profitable **triangle of trade** between **England**, **Africa**, and the **West Indies** based on the **slave trade**. Money from the trade helped England to become very rich.

Improved living standards

One of the effects of Elizabeth's policies was **improved living standards,** as is described by this eyewitness:

> In noblemen's houses it is not rare to see rich tapestries, silverware and other plate. In the houses of knights, gentlemen and merchants you can see tapestries, pewter, brass, fine linen and costly cupboards with pewter. Many farmers also have beds with silk hangings, tables with fine linen. Old men say that three things have altered most in their memory. (A description of England, William Harrison, 1577)

The increased wealth of the country enabled beautiful Tudor houses to be built, such as Hardwick Hall in Derbyshire. The arts flourished, notably with the plays of William Shakespeare and the building of the famous Globe theatre.

London's water supply was the wonder of Elizabethan times according to a contemporary source:

> Spring water is enclosed in stone cisterns in different parts of the town. It is let off into iron-bound buckets which men carry to houses and sell. (Travels in England, Thomas Platter, 1599).

Fig. 2.14 A 1996 reconstruction of the Globe Theatre.

The rhyme 'Hark, hark, the dogs do bark, the beggars are coming to town' comes from this period.

However, **Elizabeth's policies** towards the **poor people** of England were often cruel. The poor were treated much more harshly than they had been by the monks and nuns before the Reformation (see topic 1.5).

People could become poor for many reasons, such as high food prices due to bad harvests, sickness, childbirth, injury in war, old age, being thrown off the land by the landlord, or being widowed or orphaned.

Poor people often became '**vagabonds**', roaming the streets looking for food or work, or robbing.

The Elizabethan **Poor Law** was passed in 1601 to try to control the rising numbers of poor people and it lasted until 1834.

Depending on your situation, you would have had different views about life under Elizabeth. Catholics, Puritans, ordinary Protestants, poor people, rich people – they all had different experiences.

- Begging was banned, and when people lost their jobs they had to go back to their home parish.
- Unemployed people who refused to work were sent to prison workhouses.
- Beggars' backs became bloody, as they were whipped out of town.

Key Point

Elizabeth's England had its bad side as well as its good side.

Progress Check

1 Who did Elizabeth encourage to trade with other nations?
2 Name two rival European countries in the 16th century.
3 What was the name given to the system of trade between Britain, Africa and America?
4 What terrible trade did British merchants take part in?
5 Name a famous writer of plays in Elizabeth's reign.
6 What happened to living standards for merchants under Elizabeth?
7 When was the harsh Poor Law written?

1. Merchant companies. 2. Portugal and Spain. 3. Triangle of trade. 4. Slavery. 5 Shakespeare. 6. They rose. 7. 1601.

2.7 Why did the Stuart monarchy allow England to fall into Civil War in 1642?

After studying this topic you should be able to explain:

- how King James I quarrelled with Parliament over religion and the rights of kings
- how King Charles I split with Parliament over taxation and religion
- when the English Civil War became inevitable
- who were the main leaders of the Parliamentary rebellion against Charles I
- whether you think that King Charles I or the MPs were more to blame for the war.

> The causes of the Civil War were long-term, medium-term and short-term.

The **Stuart kings James I (1603–1625)** and **Charles I (1625–1647) quarrelled with Parliament**. By 1642, relationships between the monarchy and most members of Parliament had broken down so badly that both sides formed armies and fought a vicious **Civil War**, ending with the execution of Charles I.

King James quarrels with Parliament

James VI of Scotland became **King James I of England** because Elizabeth had no heir (see topic 2.6).

James I **quarrelled with Parliament** over his royal claim to the '**divine right of kings**'. His idea of divine right was expressed to MPs in 1610:

> *Kings are God's lieutenants. They exercise a manner of divine power on Earth. To dispute what God may do is blasphemy: so it is sedition for subjects to dispute what a King may do.*
> (James I to the Commons, 1610)

Fig. 2.15 James I.

James I also argued with Parliament over **religion**. He quarrelled with the English Puritans, the people who wanted to strip away all the remains of the Catholic religion they saw in the Church of England that Elizabeth I had established (see topic 2.3).

James objected to Puritan demands to get rid of the **bishops** who governed the Church of England.

At the 1604 Hampton Court Conference, James told them:

As I have said before, 'No bishop, no King.' I will make these men conform themselves, or I will harry them out of my kingdom. (An account of the Hampton Court Conference, 14 January 1604, by William Barlow, later Bishop of Rochester)

> Tensions between the crown and Parliament were over money, religion and personalities.

Puritans feared that James I was secretly a Catholic. He was the son of Mary Queen of Scots (see topic 2.4).

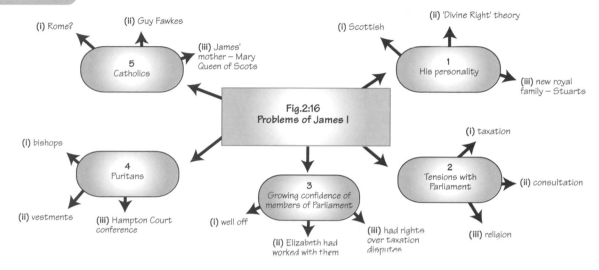

(i) Rome?

(ii) Guy Fawkes

(iii) James' mother – Mary Queen of Scots

5 Catholics

(i) Scottish

(ii) 'Divine Right' theory

(iii) new royal family – Stuarts

1 His personality

Fig.2:16
Problems of James I

(i) bishops

4 Puritans

(ii) vestments

(iii) Hampton Court conference

3 Growing confidence of members of Parliament

(i) well off

(ii) Elizabeth had worked with them

(iii) had rights over taxation disputes

(i) taxation

2 Tensions with Parliament

(ii) consultation

(iii) religion

> **Key Point**
>
> The Stuart kings did not seem to understand the lessons learned by the wiser kings in the Middle Ages (see Chapter 1), that the country could not be run as a kind of dictatorship.

The descent into civil war

Without the foolish policies of Charles I and the opposition of important MPs and groups of people outside Parliament such as Scottish Protestants, there would not have been a civil war in 1642.

Fig. 2.17 Leading MP John Pym.

Fig. 2.18 Edward Coke, who led the opposition to Charles I.

The timeline below shows how the country accelerated into civil war under Charles I.

1625 **Charles I marries a Catholic** from France, Henrietta Maria.	This annoys and frightens Protestants.
1628–1629 Charles collects taxes without permission to pay for failed wars against Spain and France. The tax is called **'ship money'** as it is to pay for a navy. He then **sends Parliament home** and rules alone.	This angers the merchants and the land-owners, who send the MPs back to Parliament in a very angry mood. **Coke, Pym** and **Hampden** are the leaders of the MPs. More people in England become very angry with the King. People **refuse to pay the taxes**.
1637 **Scottish Protestants rebel** against a **Prayer Book** which is too Catholic for their taste.	Many MPs in England agree with the Scottish Protestants. They hate the 'Romish' Archbishop Laud who they believe is trying to make England and Scotland's churches too much like the Catholic Church.
1640 Charles **recalls Parliament** because he needs money to fight the Scottish Protestants. He charges a new tax, **'coat and conduct money'**, to pay for soldiers' uniforms and equipment.	Angry MPs in what became known as the '**Long Parliament**' demand that, in return for the money, Laud and the King's advisor, Strafford, be arrested and that the King must reform the way he governs. Strafford is executed.
November 1641 MPs publish the **Grand Remonstrance** and Parliament votes by a majority of one to demand that the King listen to councillors appointed by MPs. **Charles refuses to obey Parliament.**	There is a growing **demand for control by Parliament of the King.**
November 1641 **Irish Rebellion against Protestants.**	English Protestants suspect Charles of being in league with the Catholics who have massacred the Protestants in Ireland.
January 1642 **Charles tries to arrest the five MPs** who had led the rebellion in Parliament.	The MPs have been warned and flee the House of Commons in boats on the river Thames. Charles says, *The birds have flown* and the Speaker of the House refuses to help the King.
February 1642 MPs vote to **throw the bishops out** of the House of Lords. This shows that the MPs are dominated by **Puritans**.	This worries non-Puritans and the King, who believe in a national Anglican Church.
March 1642 **Parliament takes control of the army** to stop Charles sending the soldiers off to wars they do not support.	This means that the **King has lost control of the country** – he has no power.
June 1642 A majority of MPs vote for the **Nineteen Propositions**. These give **control of politics to Parliament**, with the King as a ceremonial figure (a system that continues today).	Supporters of the King leave Parliament to form an army and Parliament also forms an army. In each county people choose whether to join the Royal Army or the Parliamentary Army. Families are often divided.

Key Point

As with the 1381 Peasants' Revolt (see Chapter 1), money was a big factor behind protests against the government.

Progress Check

1 What was the theory by which James I and Charles I governed England?
2 What was the problem with Charles I's wife?
3 Why did the Scottish Protestants rebel in 1637?
4 Name three leaders of the opposition to Charles I.
5 Who refused to help Charles I arrest the leading MPs in 1642?
6 Which religious group increasingly dominated Parliament in the 1640s?
7 Name the document of 1641 that attacked the King's government.
8 Which Parliamentary document finally started the Civil War?

1. The divine right of kings. 2. She was Catholic. 3. They disliked the Prayer Book, which was too Catholic. 4. Hampden, Pym and Coke. 5. The Speaker of the House of Commons. 6. Puritans. 7. The Grand Remonstrance. 8. The Nineteen Propositions.

2.8 What were the causes and effects of the execution of Charles I in 1649?

After studying this topic you should understand:

- who belonged to the Royalist Army and who belonged to the Parliamentary Army
- why Oliver Cromwell was a great general
- why the Battle of Marston Moor was so important
- how Charles I came to be put on trial
- why Charles was sentenced to death
- who ruled England from 1649–1660
- how the Royalists got their revenge in 1660.

The defeat of the King's armies in the Civil War, 1642–46

Fig. 2.19 Charles I.

Charles I left London after failing to arrest the five leading MPs (see topic 2.7). He went north, hoping to find more supporters as he moved further away from London. In August 1642 he raised his standard at Nottingham and asked the people to follow him. Parliament began to raise an army in London and in the east of the country.

Most of **Charles' supporters were noblemen** and their followers; they were good horsemen (and were called **Cavaliers**). They were trained in using weapons so that they won most of the early battles.

Parliament's support came from **townspeople**, **small farmers**, and **merchants**. They were called **Roundheads**. Parliament's control of the navy made it difficult for the King to get supplies from France. This meant that the longer the war went on, the stronger Parliament's position became.

Key Point

Oliver Cromwell is one of the 'key individuals' who changed history, and his career affects our lives today.

Without Oliver Cromwell, it is unlikely that King Charles would have lost the war. Charles would then not have been killed. This is an example of key individuals changing history.

Oliver Cromwell was leader of the Roundheads. After early defeats by the Cavaliers, Cromwell trained a '**New Model Army**'. He insisted on discipline, training and the preaching of the idea that God supported their Puritan faith. Cromwell's troops won an important victory at Marston Moor in July 1644, when they defeated Charles' best general Prince Rupert, who was forced into hiding.

On 5 May 1646, **Charles was captured** by the Puritan Scottish army and imprisoned at Carisbrooke Castle on the Isle of Wight.

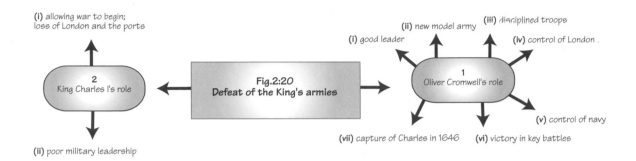

(i) allowing war to begin; loss of London and the ports

2 King Charles I's role

Fig.2:20 **Defeat of the King's armies**

1 Oliver Cromwell's role

(i) good leader

(ii) new model army

(iii) disciplined troops

(iv) control of London

(v) control of navy

(vii) capture of Charles in 1646

(vi) victory in key battles

(ii) poor military leadership

> Notice that Charles made many mistakes in his dealings with Parliament.

Cromwell negotiated with the imprisoned King Charles in 1648 at **Carisbrooke Castle** to end the war. **Charles rejected Cromwell's offer** that the King should rule with Parliament's consent. But Charles made a deal with the Scots, who wanted to have a weak king rather than a strong Cromwell in power in England.

Cromwell defeated the Scots at Preston (1648) and King Charles was arrested and put on trial for treason.

The trial and execution of Charles

Fig. 2.21 Charles I on trial.

The trial began on 29 January 1649. Only 68 out of 135 Commissioners turned up for the trial. The rest stayed in their country houses to escape the choice between Cromwell and the King!

The **accusations against Charles I** in 1649 were very powerful.

> *Charles Stuart, King of England … traitorously waged war against Parliament and the people. … He is therefore, a tyrant, a traitor, and a murderer, and an enemy to the Commonwealth of England.*

Stupidly, **Charles denied the court's right to try him**. This annoyed the Commissioners.

> *I wish to know by what power I am called hither. I would know by what lawful authority. Remember I am your King, your lawful King. … I say, think well on it, before you go from one sin to a greater one. I have a trust given me by God, by old and lawful descent.*
> (Charles I to his judges)

Key Point

Charles' belief in the 'divine right of kings' was outdated and unacceptable to most MPs.

Fig. 2.22 The execution of the King.

After the trial, Charles was found **guilty** and sentenced to be **executed on 30 January 1649**.

An eyewitness at Charles I's execution described the moving scene:

> *I stood amongst the crowd in the street before Whitehall gate where the scaffold was erected and saw what was done ... The blow I saw given and can truly say, with a sad heart: ... there was such a groan by the thousands, as I never heard before and desire I may never hear again.*
> (Diaries, Philip Henry, edited in 1882)

After the execution people came to dip their handkerchiefs in the King's blood and to take hairs from his head and his beard. On 31 January 1649, Charles' head was sewn back on the body and he was buried in Windsor Castle.

Supporters of the King regarded the dead King as a **martyr**, but supporters of Cromwell regarded him as a **traitor**.

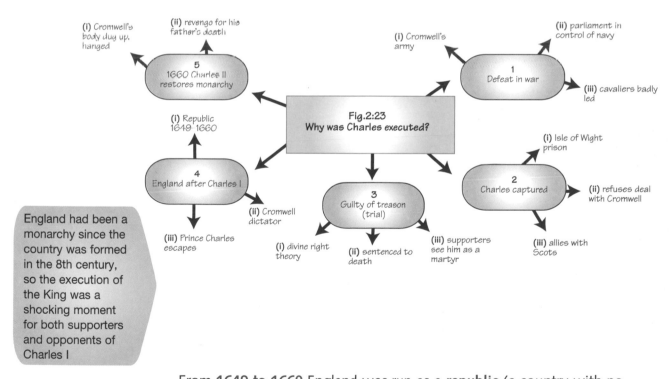

England had been a monarchy since the country was formed in the 8th century, so the execution of the King was a shocking moment for both supporters and opponents of Charles I

'Revolutions devour their children.'

From **1649 to 1660** England was run as a **republic** (a country with no monarch). **Cromwell became the leader** of the country; he died in 1658.

When Charles I's son was given the throne in 1660, and became **King Charles II**, the supporters of the monarchy got their revenge on Cromwell and his supporters. The bodies of Oliver Cromwell and the leading Commissioners were dug up and hanged on the gallows at Tyburn Hill. Other supporters of Cromwell who were still alive were tried and found guilty of **regicide** (killing a king).

Key Point The execution of the King of England was imitated by the French in 1793 (see Chapter 3).

Fig. 2.24 The execution of the regicides.

 Progress Check

1 In what part of the country did Charles I have most support?
2 Where did Parliament have most of its support?
3 Who created the 'New Model Army'?
4 What were the Royalist soldiers called?
5 What were the Parliamentary soldiers called?
6 When was King Charles executed?
7 What did his supporters call Charles I after he died?
8 When England lost her monarchy, what did the country become?

1. The north. 2. London and the east. 3. Oliver Cromwell. 4. Cavaliers. 5. Roundheads. 6. 30 January 1649. 7. A martyr. 8. A republic.

2.9 How good a ruler was Cromwell (1649–1660)?

After studying this topic you should be able to:

- describe the positive aspects of Cromwell's rule
- describe the negative aspects of his rule
- assess whether the negatives outweigh the positives
- explain why some people admire Cromwell
- explain why some people hate Cromwell
- appreciate the long-term effects of Cromwell's career.

Between 1649 and 1660 England was a **republic**, for the first time in her history. The most important force in the country was the **New Model Army** led by **Oliver Cromwell**. People who dislike Cromwell point to his cruelty, while other people say that he was trying to make the country safe and avoid a new civil war.

Dealing with the Irish rebellions

Cromwell's first problem was how to stop the **rebellions in Ireland** against English rule. **Irish Catholics supported Prince Charles**, the son of the dead King.

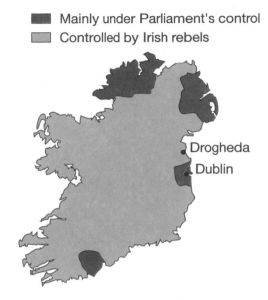

■ Mainly under Parliament's control
■ Controlled by Irish rebels

Drogheda
Dublin

Fig. 2.25 Ireland in 1649.

In response, Cromwell took 12,000 soldiers to Ireland and crushed the Irish army at Drogheda.

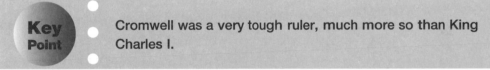

Key Point

Cromwell was a very tough ruler, much more so than King Charles I.

Cromwell's letter about the massacre at Drogheda of September 1649 is a very valuable source.

The enemy were about 3000 strong in the town. They made a stout resistance. … God gave a new courage to our men: they entered again and beat the enemy from their defences. … I believe we put to the sword the whole number of defendants. … This is the righteous judgement of God upon these barbarous wretches who dipped their hands in innocent blood. (Letter from Cromwell, 16 September 1649)

> Cromwell's treatment of Ireland started the long period of conflict between the two nations.

Cromwell **took almost all the land from the Irish Catholics** and gave it to his **English Protestant supporters**. This meant the **Irish Catholics** became very **poor** and very **anti-English**.

Crushing the Scottish Royalists

Cromwell then smashed the Scottish supporters of Charles I at the **Battle of Dunbar** in September 1650. His words are a valuable guide to his methods of keeping power.

The enemy's numbers were great – about 6000 horse and 16,000 foot at least: ours, about 7500 foot and 3500 horse. … The horse beat back all opposition, charging through the enemy's horse and foot... It became a total rout – about 3000 slain.
(Letter from Cromwell to Speaker of Parliament, 4 September 1650)

By 1653 Cromwell had **successfully imposed his rule on Scotland**, so it would not threaten England. He then turned to England to try to bring law and order to the country after the chaos of civil war.

Cromwell's rule over England

Fig. 2.26 Oliver Cromwell.

- In 1653, **Cromwell's army dismissed the Rump Parliament** (the MPs who were left after all the Royalists had gone) because Cromwell thought the MPs had not been effective.
- After new elections, the new Parliament named Cromwell as **Lord Protector** for life.
- Cromwell had to deal with the **Levellers**, led by **John Liliburne**, who thought that everyone had the right to vote. But Cromwell's loyal troops crushed them in May 1649. Four of the Levellers' leaders were hanged. Cromwell and his supporters were landlords and did not want the ordinary people to have power.
- In 1655 Parliament criticised Cromwell's decision to allow people (except Catholics) **to worship as they wished**. So he **dismissed Parliament** and named five major-generals to govern the country.
- Cromwell agreed that **religious freedom should be limited** because too many people went around 'prophesying' and stirring up the people to revolt.
- On September 3 1658 **Cromwell died**. In May 1660, after more chaos in the country, Cromwell's army and most MPs asked **Charles Stuart**, the son of King Charles I, to come back from France (where he had fled in 1649) to become king.

Historians have labelled the return of the monarchy the 'Restoration'.

After Cromwell

Key Point

Under Charles II, some of the changes made by Cromwell were reversed, but the importance of Parliament remained, so Cromwell's work was not undone.

Many of the effects of Cromwell's rule therefore survived his death and the return of the monarchy.

King Charles II was called 'The Merry Monarch' because he negotiated a deal with Parliament which **removed all the restrictions of Puritan England**. The Anglican Church was allowed to have bishops. Ministers were allowed to wear vestments in church. Dancing, singing and theatres were allowed again. Christmas Day and mince pies were brought back!

But **the power the King had held to make laws was given to Parliament**. This was the legacy of Oliver Cromwell. So when King James I tried to rule like Charles I he was removed by Parliament in a bloodless 'Glorious Revolution' (1688) and replaced by William of Orange – William III.

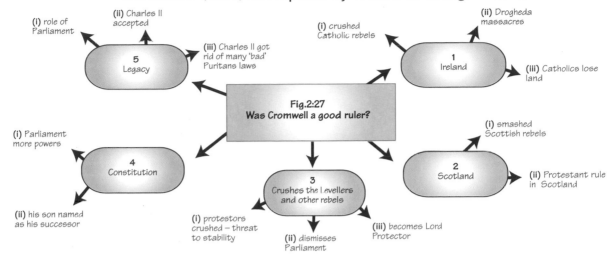

(i) role of Parliament

(ii) Charles II accepted

5 Legacy

(iii) Charles II got rid of many 'bad' Puritans laws

(i) crushed Catholic rebels

(ii) Drogheda massacres

1 Ireland

(iii) Catholics lose land

Fig.2:27 Was Cromwell a good ruler?

(i) Parliament more powers

4 Constitution

(ii) his son named as his successor

3 Crushes the Levellers and other rebels

(i) protestors crushed – threat to stability

(ii) dismisses Parliament

(iii) becomes Lord Protector

(i) smashed Scottish rebels

2 Scotland

(ii) Protestant rule in Scotland

Progress Check

1 What did England become in 1649?
2 When was the monarchy restored?
3 Against which armies did Cromwell go to war after defeating King Charles I?
4 Which protest group was crushed by Cromwell in 1649?
5 What title did Cromwell receive after defeating Charles I?
6 What was the name of the Parliament that Cromwell dismissed in 1653?
7 Name the religious group whose laws were removed in 1660.
8 Who became the next ruler of England after Cromwell died?

1. A republic. 2. 1660. 3. Ireland and Scotland. 4. Levellers 5. Lord Protector. 6. The Rump Parliament. 7. Puritans. 8. Charles Stuart (Charles II).

2.10 How was the United Kingdom created (1500–1750)?

After studying this topic you should be able to:

- **describe how the four nations within the British Isles differed in 1500**
- **describe how gradually the English exerted control over the British Isles**
- **explain why there were many rebellions against English rule**
- **explain the reasons why some people in Scotland, Wales and Ireland supported the English**
- **explain why the United Kingdom became so powerful.**

Wales is joined with England

In 1536 and 1543, the English Parliament passed the **Acts of Union**, which made Wales part of England. English law applied in Wales. Under the Acts of Union Welsh people sent MPs to the Parliament in London where the laws were made.

The **Welsh language** was still allowed to exist at this time, and a Welsh prayer book for the Church in Wales was written. However, in the 18th century the English started to suppress the Welsh language (a branch of Gaelic) by punishing people if they spoke it.

Taking control of Ireland

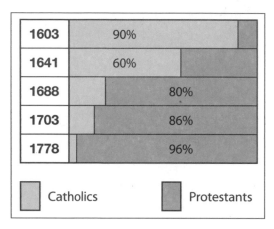

1603	90%
1641	60%
1688	80%
1703	86%
1778	96%

Catholics   Protestants

Between 1500 and 1750 the English took **control of Ireland**. Elizabeth I took Irish land and gave it to her Protestant supporters. Cromwell carried on the process of taking land from the Irish to reward his Protestant followers.

Fig. 2.28 Transfer of ownership of Irish land 1603–1778.

Key Point

> The Protestant Reformation (see Chapter 1) had not taken hold in most of Ireland, so the conquest of Ireland also involved the smashing of the Catholic religion of the Irish people.

When the **Protestant King William** (see topic 2.9) **attacked Ireland** in 1691, the Irish were further punished for their opposition to English rule. Under the **Penal Laws** Catholics in Ireland, about 85 per cent of the population, were **forbidden to vote** or to become MPs in the Dublin Parliament. They could not send their children to school, own a horse or wear a sword.

The Irish were also **forbidden to trade in wool**, in case this damaged England's wool trade. Catholics had to have wooden churches on wheels, since it was difficult to get a licence for a proper stone church from the English authorities in Ireland.

In 1801 Ireland was finally joined to Britain with the Act of Union. The Dublin Parliament was abolished.

> In 1922, Britain was forced to leave Southern Ireland. The Irish Republic was born. Six of the 32 counties of Ireland are still in the United Kingdom.

Donegal 11%
Londonderry 14%
Tyrone 4%
Antrim 41%
Fermanagh 15%
Armagh 34%
Down 26%
Sligo 58%
Leitrim 39%
Monaghan 38%
Mayo 80%
Cavan 43%
Louth 65%
Longford
Rascommon 61% 65%
W. Meath 75%
Meath 76%
Galway 91%
King's Co 46%
Kildare 49%
Dublin 46%
Queen's Co 43%
Wicklow 35%
Clare 80%
Kilkenny 58%
Carlow 72%
Tipperary 77%
Wexford 60%
Limerick 57%
Kerry 59%
Waterford 52%
Cork 65%

Fig. 2.29 The Irish counties and percentages of land allocated to Catholics.

Fig. 2.30 The Irish Parliament in session.

Dealing with Scotland

Citizenship link: since 1999 there has been a Scottish Parliament in Edinburgh. The Parliament can make laws on a wide variety of matters.

Scotland did not become part of the United Kingdom until **1707**.

The English Parliament and monarchs were pleased when Scotland united with England and Wales because Scottish people often rebelled against English monarchs.

The **Highlanders' rebellion** led to the infamous **Glencoe massacre** (1692), when thousands of Scottish highland people were slaughtered by the English and their Scottish allies, the 'Lowlanders'.

Fig. 2.31 The Scottish Act of Union being presented to Queen Anne.

However, many people in Scotland, especially the **Highlanders**, did not like English rule. James Stuart tried and failed to rouse the Scottish Highlanders in 1715, but fled to France.

Bonnie Prince Charlie did raise a huge army in 1745. He invaded England, hoping to win enough support from Catholics and others who were opposed to the Protestant monarchy, but was destroyed at **Culloden**.

> **Key Point**
>
> English cruelty to the Scottish Highlanders was shocking even to many people at the time.

Try to identify the reasons for and effects of the English conquest of Scotland.

The English then **destroyed the Highlanders' way of life**, banning their language, their kilts and their bagpipes and taking the land from them. These policies were similar to the way the Irish had been treated.

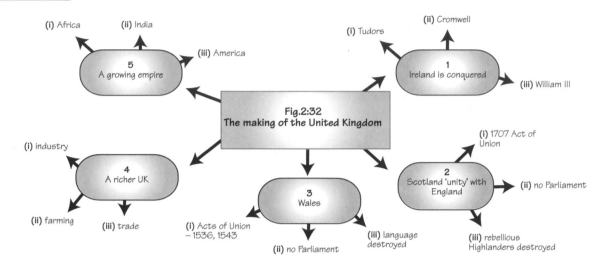

Why some supported the union

It should be remembered that many 'native' Scots, Welsh and Irish **supported the union** of their countries with England. A variety of motives explain their support:

● disappointment with the 'native' rulers of their country

● marriage or trading relationships with the English

● bribery by the English

● fear of punishment by their powerful neighbours.

The United Kingdom became the richest nation in the world during the 18th and 19th centuries, due mainly to the Industrial and Agricultural Revolutions, as we shall see in Chapter 4. The most powerful part of the United Kingdom was England.

Progress Check

1 Name the four countries of the United Kingdom in 1750.

2 When were the laws uniting England to Wales passed?

3 What happened to the Welsh legal system?

4 What name is given to the laws that crushed the Catholics in Ireland?

5 When was Scotland united to England?

6 Who led the rebellion against the English in 1745?

7 Which was the most powerful country in the United Kingdom?

1. England, Wales, Ireland, Scotland. 2. 1536 and 1543. 3. It was destroyed. 4. The Penal Laws. 5. 1707. 6. Bonnie Prince Charlie. 7. England.

The following practice questions focus on your use of knowledge and the historical skills of interpreting historical events and evaluating evidence.

Part A   Who is this person?

Identify each person described below.

1   She was Henry VIII's second wife and mother of Elizabeth I.   [1]
2   He caused a religious storm across Europe when he protested against the Catholic Church in the 16th century.   [1]
3   She was the Scottish cousin of Elizabeth I, and was executed by Elizabeth.   [1]
4   He was 'Lord Protector' of England after the English monarch, Charles I, was executed.   [1]
5   She was Elizabeth's step-sister and a devout Catholic monarch who ruled from 1553–1558.   [1]
6   He was the founder of the English Parliament in the 13th century.   [1]

Part B   What is this?

Write a few sentences to explain the meaning of the following historical ideas or events.

1   The divine right of kings.   [2]
2   The Spanish armada.   [2]
3   Parliament.   [2]
4   The Act of Supremacy.   [2]
5   The triangle of trade.   [2]
6   A primary source.   [2]

Part C   Using evidence to evaluate the rule of Oliver Cromwell.

Read the three sources and answer the questions that follow.

Source A is adapted from the words of a modern writer and politician, Roy Hattersley.

My father first told me about Oliver Cromwell. He was a Catholic and so naturally was opposed to Cromwell. I remember most strongly the accounts of his dying moments, when thunder crashed, as if God was taking revenge on his crimes. The crimes my father had in mind were, in particular, the massacre of the inhabitants of Drogheda, whose citizens revolted against Oliver Cromwell's rule after the execution of Charles I. Three years later, when Charles I's son was restored to the throne, Cromwell's corpse was dug up from Westminster Abbey and hung on a gallows at Tyburn, like a common criminal.

Yet we cannot judge great figures of the past against the standards of today. Mary and Elizabeth Tudor ordered the execution of Protestants and Catholics. Henry VIII beheaded some of his wives. Cromwell was what we today regard as brutal. But he changed England for the better and established what was the beginning of our parliamentary democracy. He was a farmer turned politician and army commander.

Source B is written by a Protestant friend of Cromwell in 1660.

Cromwell would rather have taken a shepherd's staff than the Protectorship. Nothing went more against his feelings than a show of greatness. But he saw it as necessary at the time to keep the nation from falling into extreme disorder.

Source C is written by Clarendon, a friend of Charles II.

This man, against the desires of all noble persons, took the throne of three kingdoms, without the name of king, but with greater authority and power than had been claimed by any king.

Answer the following questions on these sources.

1   What can you learn from these sources about Cromwell's achievements?   [5]
2   In what ways does Source B back up or contradict Source A?
    Explain your answer.   [5]
3   How does Source C differ from Source B? Why do they have different points
    of view about Cromwell?   [5]
4   How useful are these sources to historians assessing the contribution of Oliver
    Cromwell to the development of Britain?   [5]

Part D   A short obituary of Elizabeth I

Imagine that you are an Elizabethan and you have just heard of the death of
Queen Elizabeth I. Using the text and the extracts in topics 2.3 to 2.6, write an
obituary of the Queen. Explain in your obituary who would have supported her
and who would have opposed her during different times in her reign.
Conclude your piece of work by saying whether you think that her strengths
are more impressive than her weaknesses.   [10]

3 The French Revolution

The topics covered in this chapter are:

- **The long-term causes of the French Revolution**
- **The first stage of the French Revolution, 1787–9**
- **Revolution spreads in France**
- **The King is executed**
- **The short-term effects of the French Revolution**
- **The long-term effects of the French Revolution**

3.1 What were the long-term causes of the French Revolution in 1789?

After studying this topic you should be able to:

- **understand what the King and Queen of France were like**
- **describe who the 'three estates' represented**
- **explain why many people were angry with the government of France in 1780**
- **understand the effects of the American Revolution on many French people**
- **appreciate the importance of the ideas of Jean Jacques Rousseau.**

> Long-term causes are causes which build up over a long period of time. For example, in your life, there have been influences on you over the years since you were born.

a The *ancien regime* was **old-fashioned** and **unjust** and was ripe for change. **King Louis XVI** and his infamous wife Marie Antoinette ruled France. The King had total power. He regarded himself as God's representative on Earth and lived in luxury in palaces like Versailles.

b The King presided over a country which was divided into '**three estates**'.

- The **first estate** was the **clergy of the Catholic Church**: the bishops and the parish priests. There were about 100,000 of them. Most bishops were very rich land-owners, and the peasants paid taxes (tithes) to them.

- The **second estate** was the **nobility**. There were about 400,000 nobles, who owned most of the land in France. They owned *chateaux* (castles) and were paid tithes by the peasants, as rent for the use of their land.

● The **third estate** was 'the people'. They included business people, professional people, town workers, rural peasants and landless labourers. There were about 23 million of them.

Key Point

France was a deeply divided country before the Revolution and the divisions were stirring up many troubles for the French monarchy.

'Middle class' refers to people who are not very rich, but not poor either. Lawyers, bankers, shopkeepers and factory-owners are middle class.

c By the 1780s, the middle class was growing. Many French businessmen and professional people began to question the way the country was governed.

They were influenced by Jean Jacques Rousseau's book *The Social Contract*. The following extract inspired many people of the third estate to want to change the way France was ruled.

Man is born free. No man has any natural authority over others; force does not give anyone that right. The power to make laws belongs to the people and only to the people. (A pamphlet, banned by the French government in 1775, commenting on *The Social Contract* (1762), Jean Jacques Rousseau)

d The **American Revolution of 1776** also inspired some people in France to fight for their freedom. The British were thrown out of America by George Washington's armies, which included many French volunteers. Inspired by the Americans, many books were written encouraging people to revolt against the way that France was organised.

You should be able to compare the causes of the French Revolution with the causes of the English Civil War. Taxation, anger with the government and new ideas all played their part.

e **Peasants** were increasingly **angry** with the clergy and the nobility, according to an eyewitness:

'The taxes and the feudal dues are crushing us.'
(*Travels in France*, Arthur Young, 1792)

There was a growing list of complaints by the nobles and by the 'third estate' against taxes the King's government was trying to make them pay.

Key Point

A combination of money problems and new ideas of liberty were the basic threats to the old French system of royal rule.

Progress Check

1 Name the King and Queen of France in 1780.
2 How many 'estates' were there in France?
3 What was the name of the tax that peasants had to pay?
4 Who belonged to the 'first estate'?
5 Who belonged to the 'second estate'?
6 Who belonged the 'third estate'?
7 Which group was at the bottom of the 'third estate'?

1. Louis XVI and Marie Antoinette. 2. Three. 3. Tithes. 4. The clergy. 5. The nobility. 6. 'The people'. 7. The peasants.

3.2 The first stage of the French Revolution, 1787–9

After studying this topic you should be able to:

- understand the financial problems facing France on the eve of Revolution
- understand the problems to do with the harvest in 1787
- explain why the King called the Estates-General meeting
- appreciate the mistakes made by the King at the meeting of the estates
- describe the importance of individuals such as Mirabeau and Abbé Sièyes
- understand the importance of the famous 'tennis court meeting'.

'Revolution' is defined as the transfer of power from one group to another. This happened in France when the King lost his power and his life.

By 1787 the French government was **bankrupt**, as the figures show:

Income	560 million livres
Spending	630 million livres
Total debt	4000 million livres

France had spent a great deal of money fighting wars against Britain. Some French people accused Queen Marie Antoinette of spending too much money.

The harvest problem, 1787–9

In the three years 1787–9, heavy rain, hard winters and hot dry summers led to three very **poor harvests**. Farmers and peasants had **smaller incomes** and town workers had to pay **higher prices** for their **food**. Town workers were also being made **unemployed** as the rural workers had less money to buy goods made in the towns.

Key Point

It is very dangerous for any government when the people suffer hunger.

The King and the Estates-General

In August 1788 the desperate King decided to call the **Estates-General** – a gathering of representatives from all three estates. This had last happened in 1614. The three estates met in separate buildings, on **4 May 1789**.

If the King had not called the meeting, would there have been a revolution in 1789? We will never know.

- The King hoped the Estates-General would approve new taxes.
- The nobles (along with the clergy) hoped for concessions from the King.
- The middle class hoped to create an English-style democracy.

● The peasants hoped for an end to the suffering caused by high taxes and a series of bad harvests.

The King's mistakes, May–June 1789

This shows the human side of history, which is very easy to overlook.

● The King summoned the three estates to meet at his palace at Versailles.

● He failed to present the meeting with real suggestions for improving France, so that the people of the three estates were left to think up their own ideas.

● He was preoccupied with his dying son. He did not focus on France's problems.

The National Assembly

A radical is someone who wants to change a country at its root.

The National Assembly began on 19 June 1789.

Radical nobles such as **Mirabeau** and **radical priests** such as **Abbé Sièyes** were responsible for leading the Assembly and deciding that they should draw up a **constitution** showing how France was to be governed.

Key Point
The King was threatened by the fact that his enemies began to unite.

Notice that these key dates are turning points in French history.

On 20 June the members of this (illegal) Assembly met in the royal tennis court at Versailles to swear an oath that they would not leave until the King met their demands. He agreed to the setting up of a National Assembly (parliament).

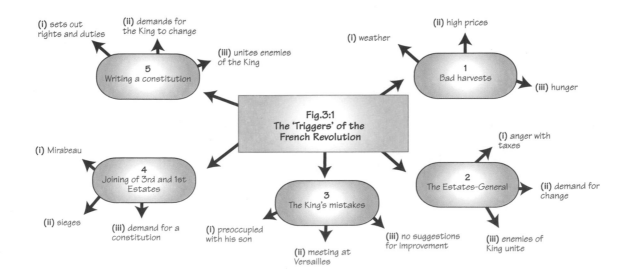

(i) sets out rights and duties
(ii) demands for the King to change
(iii) unites enemies of the King

5 Writing a constitution

(i) weather
(ii) high prices
(iii) hunger

1 Bad harvests

Fig.3:1 The 'Triggers' of the French Revolution

(i) Mirabeau
(ii) sieges
(iii) demand for a constitution

4 Joining of 3rd and 1st Estates

(i) preoccupied with his son
(ii) meeting at Versailles

3 The King's mistakes

(iii) no suggestions for improvement

(i) anger with taxes
(ii) demand for change
(iii) enemies of King unite

2 The Estates-General

3.3 Why did revolution spread in France from July to September 1789?

After studying this topic you should be able to understand:

- why there were riots in Paris in July 1789
- the importance of the laws passed by the National Assembly in 1789
- the impact of the new French constitution
- the importance of the *Declaration of the Rights of Man*
- what happened to the old feudal taxes in the Legal Revolution.

Violent revolutionary mobs take control in July 1789

The Paris mob, hungry because of poor harvests, and impatient, took the law into its own hands. On **14 July 1789** the mob attacked the prison in Paris, the **Bastille**, freed its seven prisoners and stole guns and ammunition.

Throughout France, the **peasants**, too, had become impatient. They took part in a widespread but **unorganised series of attacks** on the *chateaux* and palaces of their feudal lords.

Arthur Young, an eyewitness, recorded these violent events in his tour of France 1787–92:

> The Revolution kept on going, like a wheel turning. It 'devoured its children' because many of the people who started the revolution were killed themselves.

The whole country is in the greatest agitation. Many chateaux have been burned and others plundered. The Lords hunted down like beasts. (*Travels in France*, Arthur Young, 1792)

Key Point

Once the National Assembly started passing laws, no one could stop it. The elected members of the Assembly had the power to change France and did not want to lose it.

The Legal Revolution, August to September 1789

4 August 1789   The Assembly passed a law ending all feudal powers and unjust taxation.

12–26 August 1789   The Assembly issued the *Declaration of the Rights of Man*.

The **Declaration of the Rights of Man**, is a powerful source. It is very useful for historians writing about the Revolution.

Men are born equal and remain free and equal in rights, which are liberty, property, security and resistance to oppression. Liberty is being able to do whatever does not harm others.

The law should express the will of the people. All citizens have a right to take part … in the making of the law. Every citizen can talk, write and publish freely, unless this liberty is abused in a way which breaks the law. (*Declaration of the Rights of Man*, 27 August 1789).

The Assembly voted to write a French constitution to organise a 'government of liberty'.

Fig. 3.2 The members of the three estates go in procession to Versailles to hammer out a new way of life and government for France.

> **Key Point**
>
> A constitution sets out the way a country is ruled.

The new constitution

- A new **National Convention** was to be elected by men who were well off enough to pay taxes.
- A **new currency and taxation system** was introduced to cover the whole of France.
- **The Church lost its land** to the state, and **lost its power to tax** its tenants (tithes).
- **Priests** had to be **elected** and make **oaths of loyalty** to France and not to the Pope.

There were losers and winners from the years of the Revolution.

3.4 Why was the King executed by the revolutionaries on 21 January 1793?

After studying this topic you should understand:

- **how King Louis XVI and his wife contributed to their deaths**
- **how military defeat contributed to the King's execution**
- **the events that led to the arrest of the King**
- **why he was found guilty at his trial**
- **how he went to his death**
- **how people reacted to his death.**

The reign of Louis XVI

Compare the events surrounding the executions of the French King and the English King 140 years before (see topic 2.8).

The personality of the King and Queen made it difficult for people to love them. Like his father and grandfather, Louis XVI believed that he was God's servant and that this gave him the power to make laws.

Louis was dominated by his strong-willed wife, Marie Antoinette, the sister of the Emperor of Austria. She was the subject of many rumours about her lavish spending on clothes and jewels. She interfered in Louis's attempts to govern the country.

Louis XVI's flight to Varennes, June 1791

During the night of 20–21 June, Louis and his family, in disguise and carrying false papers of identity, left Paris.

Unfortunately for Louis, he was recognised along the route, and at

Varennes a mob prevented the coach from proceeding. He was brought back to Paris (25 June).

The King takes an oath of loyalty

A constitutional monarch is a monarch who abides by laws made in a parliament.

After a long debate the National Assembly decided to keep the monarch. The King took an oath of loyalty to the constitution on 3 September 1791 (see topic 3.3), but many people in the Assembly and throughout France knew the King did not believe in the new system of government. The King's supporters claimed that he was trying to behave like a constitutional monarch, by agreeing to sign the decrees of the National Assembly and by refusing to order his troops to massacre the protesting mobs.

Fig. 3.3 The King and his family being brought back to Paris.

Key Point

The King brought death on his own head, as King Charles I had done in England (see Chapter 2).

Defeat in war against the Austrians, April to August 1792

The war against Austria was started by the French National Assembly. Unluckily for the King, many people in France blamed him for the defeat and for the **higher food prices** and **starvation** that the war caused. People thought the French King wanted the French army to lose.

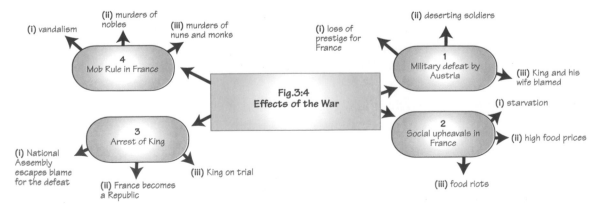

The arrest and trial of the King

On 10 August 1791, mobs of starving people, supported by soldiers, stormed Louis XVI's Tuileries Palace and arrested him. On 21 September 1791, the National Assembly announced that France was a **republic**. The 22 September was 'the first day of liberty'.

On 26 December 1792 the 749 members of the Convention put the King on trial. The King had lawyers, but he could not call witnesses. He was charged with **bankrupting** France, that he was **disloyal** to the new constitution and that he was **plotting against the Revolution**.

Was the King's execution inevitable? What do you think?

Louis denied the charges, but he was found guilty by 693 votes to nil. By a majority of just 374 votes to 321 the Convention court voted that Louis should be **executed**, by **guillotine**.

Fig. 3.5 The trial of Louis XVI.

The execution of the King, 21 January 1793

The King was very brave as he went to his death. He attended mass at 6 am and was taken to the Place de la Revolution at 8 am. It was very cold. All the shops were closed and soldiers guarded the streets. Louis arrived at the spot where he was to be executed at 10 am and at 10.22 he was dead.

The King's corpse was thrown into an unmarked grave. Revolutionaries shouted *Long live liberty! Long live equality! Long live the Republic!*

Regicide means the killing of a king.

Supporters of the King tried to flee France, but many were caught and also executed.

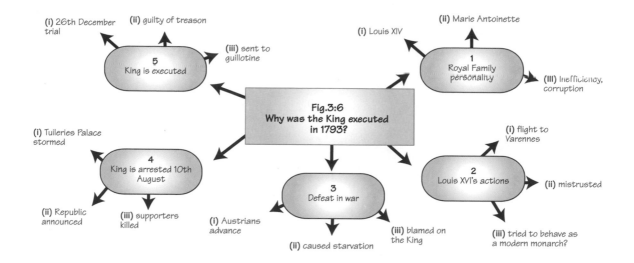

Fig.3:6
Why was the King executed in 1793?

1 Royal Family personality
(i) Louis XIV
(ii) Marie Antoinette
(iii) Inefficiency, corruption

2 Louis XVI's actions
(i) flight to Varennes
(ii) mistrusted
(iii) tried to behave as a modern monarch?

3 Defeat in war
(i) Austrians advance
(ii) caused starvation
(iii) blamed on the King

4 King is arrested 10th August
(i) Tuileries Palace stormed
(ii) Republic announced
(iii) supporters killed

5 King is executed
(i) 26th December trial
(ii) guilty of treason
(iii) sent to guillotine

Key Point

As with the English King Charles I, the belief in divine right to rule was unacceptable to most people.

Progress Check

1 What did the King try to do in June 1791?
2 For what military defeat was the King blamed in 1791?
3 Where was the King arrested in August 1791?
4 Who put the King on trial in December 1792?
5 By what majority did the court vote for the King to be executed?
6 When was the King of France executed?

1. Escape France. 2. Defeat by the Austrians. 3. His palace. 4. The National Convention.
5. Majority of 53 out of 695. 6. 21 January 1792.

3.5 What were the short-term effects of the French Revolution (1793–95)?

After studying this topic you should be able to understand:

- the effects on France of the Committee for Public Safety
- why the 'terror' was launched against the aristocrats
- the role of key individuals in revolutionary France
- how there was a kind of civil war in France, 1793–1795
- how the revolutionaries themselves were 'devoured'
- the role of Napoleon Bonaparte in stopping the Revolution.

> These were the key people in France who replaced the old government of France under the King.

Danton kept the Paris mob happy. He paid people who went to public meetings of the Committee.

Robespierre was the Committee's main public speaker. He made sure that the Convention let the Committee get on with the task of saving France.

'Death to the aristocrats!'

The '**terror**' took revenge on old France. The **guillotining** of **nobles**, **failed generals** and anyone thought to be a **royalist** accelerated as the revolutionaries wanted to get rid of the *ancien regime*.

Catholicism was attacked because it had supported the King. Christianity was 'abolished', thousands of churches were closed and many priests were executed.

Key Point

There were many French people who opposed the Revolution, but they were crushed.

Anti-revolutionary forces are crushed

Anti-revolutionary forces were crushed in 1793 by the Convention.

- **The Girondists** in Bordeaux – who were moderates and who resented the way in which 'the tail' (Paris) was 'wagging the dog' (France) – were killed by government troops.
- **Royalists** who rebelled in Toulon joined with moderates in Marseilles

but they failed to reverse the Revolution.

● In **the Vendée,** peasants rose in defence of their Church and baby King, as can be seen in this account:

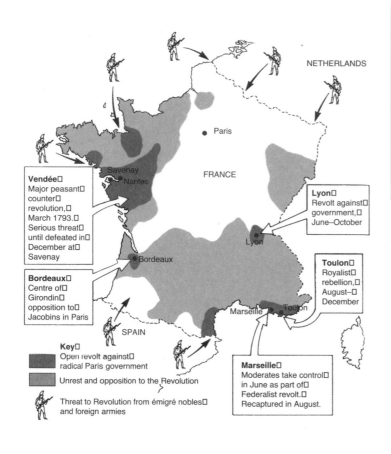

Fig. 3.7 The Revolution under threat.

The Revolution devours its children, July 1793 to July 1794

The old revolutionary Marat was stabbed to death in the bath by Charlotte Corday, because she believed that Marat was a dangerous revolutionary.

A new Committee for Public Safety was set up. Robespierre dominated the Committee and ordered the death of old revolutionaries like Danton and thousands of his allies.

The Revolution is stopped – July 1794 to October 1795

Robespierre was also executed.

Barras, as head of the Directorate, had a young officer, **Napoleon Bonaparte,** as his subordinate. When the Jacobin mobs attacked the Convention in an attempt at another cycle of revolution, Napoleon ordered his artillery to fire on the mob, which Napoleon called a whiff of grapeshot. The Jacobins were massacred.

Napoleon Bonaparte was really the creator of modern France. He was brought to power by the Revolution, but he stopped the Revolution to save France.

In return, Napoleon was made **commander of the home army** – his first step on the road to power. Napoleon brought law and order back to France, to the delight of most people in France, who feared for their lives and their property.

Key Point

Napoleon Bonaparte was the most important person to come out of the events of the Revolution.

Fig. 3.8 Napoleon Bonaparte.

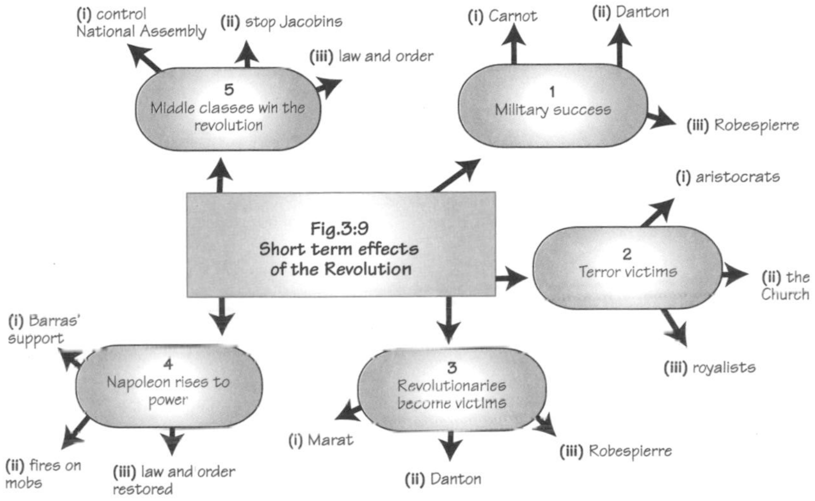

Fig.3:9 Short term effects of the Revolution

5 Middle classes win the revolution
 (i) control National Assembly
 (ii) stop Jacobins
 (iii) law and order

1 Military success
 (i) Carnot
 (ii) Danton
 (iii) Robespierre

2 Terror victims
 (i) aristocrats
 (ii) the Church
 (iii) royalists

3 Revolutionaries become victims
 (i) Marat
 (ii) Danton
 (iii) Robespierre

4 Napoleon rises to power
 (i) Barras' support
 (ii) fires on mobs
 (iii) law and order restored

Progress Check

1 Where did France gain victories after the Revolution?
2 Name the three people running the Committee for Public Safety.
3 Which social class suffered the most during the terror period?
4 Name the moderate group of Revolutionaries who were also attacked in 1793.
5 In what part of France was the Church very strong?
6 Name the general who ordered his troops to fire on the mobs?
7 Which revolutionary group was crushed by the army in 1795?

1. Belgium and the Netherlands. 2. Danton, Carnot, Robespierre. 3. Aristocrats. 4. Girondists. 5. The Vendée. 6. Napoleon. 7. Jacobins.

3.6 What were the long-term effects of the French Revolution?

After studying this topic you should be able to understand:

- the problems facing France after the Revolution
- how Napoleon changed France when he became her ruler
- the long-term benefits of the Revolution for France
- the effects of the Revolution on Spain, Italy and Germany
- the effects of the Revolution on Britain.

Napoleon brings law and order to France

France was suffering as a result of ten years of war and revolution – roads were not repaired, bandits roamed freely, schools had no teachers, hospitals had no nurses, and there were royalist uprisings in 14 of the 83 departments of the country.

Napoleon returned from **wars in Egypt** in December 1799 and in Paris his loyal army took him to **total power**. He introduced a new constitution and named himself **First Consul of France**.

In 1802 Napoleon made an **agreement with the Pope**: Catholicism was accepted as the main religion of the French people.

In 1804 Napoleon announced that he was now **Emperor** and, in a ceremony attended by the Pope, crowned himself.

 Key Point In historical turning points, changes are accompanied by continuity.

Napoleon preserves many of the benefits of the Revolution

- **Feudalism was abolished**, the nobles lost their powers, the peasants were given access to **land** – and the right to pay only their fair share of taxes.
- All adult men (not women) got the **vote**, even if Napoleon did not hold any elections.
- Marriage became a civil (state) ceremony and divorce was allowed.
- The **Code Napoleon** is still the basis of the French legal system, with one set of laws for the whole country.

- Napoleon's **Legion of Honour** continues to be France's highest award for service.
- The idea of the need for a 'strong leader' remained important to France.

Fig. 3.10 The Spirit of Revolution (the people respond to the call to arms of 1793) was carved in 1833 for the Arc de Triomphe – a lasting memorial to Napoleon's (and the Revolution's) successes.

The French Revolution changes the world outside France

France was the leading power in Europe, so other people took notice of what happened and followed the French example with liberal revolutions of their own.

In Spain, for example, a pro-liberal and nationalist revolution took place in 1812. Other Europeans followed the example of the Spanish liberals – Portugal, Germany and Italy.

Writers at the time of the Revolution appreciated its importance, as seen in the quotations below:

> Revolution was supported by many people and opposed by many people.

It is one of those events which belong to the whole human race.
(Friedrich von Genitz (1764-1832)

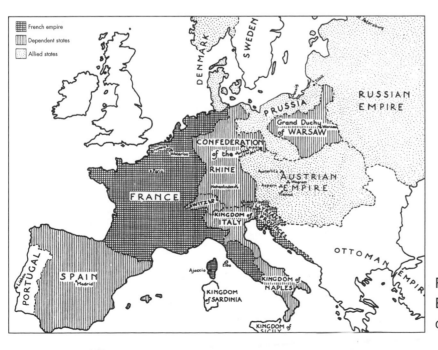

It is understood everywhere that the event of these modern ages is the French Revolution. A huge explosion, bursting through all customs.
(The English philosopher Thomas Carlyle, 1795–1881, writing in 1837)

Fig. 3.11 A map of Europe from the time of Napoleon.

Effects of the French Revolution on Britain

British aristocrats feared that the poor people would rise up in revolt, imitating what happened in France. Therefore, eventually (in the 19th century), they **gave in to demands for reform**.

In Ireland in 1798, **Wolf Tone** led an attempt to throw the British out of Ireland, having been inspired by the French concept of liberty.

The French revolutionary anthem and flag (the *Tricoleur*) were taken up as emblems by protesters in Britain, which shows how inspirational the Revolution was for many people.

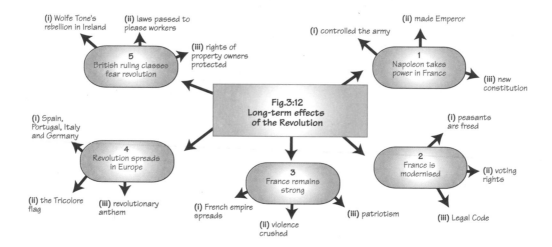

Fig.3:12 Long-term effects of the Revolution

5 British ruling classes fear revolution
- (i) Wolfe Tone's rebellion in Ireland
- (ii) laws passed to please workers
- (iii) rights of property owners protected

1 Napoleon takes power in France
- (i) controlled the army
- (ii) made Emperor
- (iii) new constitution

4 Revolution spreads in Europe
- (i) Spain, Portugal, Italy and Germany
- (ii) the Tricolore flag
- (iii) revolutionary anthem

3 France remains strong
- (i) French empire spreads
- (ii) violence crushed
- (iii) patriotism

2 France is modernised
- (i) peasants are freed
- (ii) voting rights
- (iii) Legal Code

Key Point — The French Revolution affected life in France and in lands outside France. The world became more and more inter-connected due to greater trade, travel and literacy.

Progress Check

1 What did Napoleon become in 1804?
2 What code of law did Napoleon write?
3 Who got the vote under Napoleon?
4 What social system remained abolished?
5 With whom did Napoleon sign an agreement in 1802?
6 Name two European nations where there were also revolutions in 1848.
7 Who feared revolution in Britain as a result of the French Revolution?
8 Which groups drew hope for revolution from what happened in France?

1. Emperor. 2. The Code Napoleon. 3. All men. 4. Feudalism. 5. The Church. 6. Italy and Germany. 7. Aristocrats. 8. British and Irish protesters.

The following practice questions focus on 'causes and consequences' in the knowledge and understanding strand of the History National Curriculum.

Part A   The long-term causes of revolution

Complete each of the following sentences.

1   A revolution may be defined as…   [2]
2   The royal family in France was becoming unpopular due to…   [2]
3   American revolutionary ideas were influential in France because…   [2]
4   The poverty of people in France was another problem since this led to…   [2]
5   The middle class in France was growing and they wanted to…   [2]
6   Government taxation policies were causing problems because…   [2]
7   France was divided into three classes or estates. They were…   [2]
8   All these factors made people think more about revolutionary ideas such as…   [2]

Part B   Events of the French Revolution 1787–1791

1   Rank the following reasons for the start of the French Revolution in order of their
     importance, in your opinion.   [10]
     a   Divisions in France between the rich and the poor
     b   Shortage of food because of bad harvests
     c   Foreign wars
     d   Anger of the peasants
     e   Anger of the middle class
     f   The King's mistakes
     g   The formation of the National Assembly
     h   Riots in Paris
     i   The work of the National Assembly.
2   Explain why you have chosen this order.   [5]
3   Explain how each of these factors played its part in the Revolution.   [5]
4   Explain how some of these factors are linked together.   [5]

Part C   The effects of the French Revolution

Draw a spider diagram in which you show the following effects of
the French Revolution: [10]
*   The execution of the King
*   The victims of the Revolution
*   The rise and fall of revolutionaries
*   The rise of Napoleon Bonaparte
*   The long-term benefits of the Revolution for France
*   The impact of the Revolution on Europe.

4 Britain 1750–1900

The topics covered in this chapter are:

- Growing population and towns
- Agricultural modernisation
- The first Industrial Revolution
- Factory and public health reforms
- Violent protest
- True democracy not established in Britain by 1900
- Women's progress in Victorian England

4.1 Growing population and towns

After studying this topic you should be able to:

- explain how towns grew in size during the Industrial Revolution
- give examples of the places where the new industrial towns developed
- understand the main causes of rising population
- explain why the death rate fell over the period
- explain why the birth rate rose over the period
- understand the effects of the rising population
- compare how Britain looked in 1750 with how it looked in 1900.

Study the maps on the next page, comparing the population spread in England in 1700 to that in 1901.

 Key Point The growth of towns during the Industrial Revolution built upon the growth of towns in the Middle Ages (see Chapter 1).

In 1700 the most populated areas were the south, the south-west and East Anglia. Even there, the population was small. By 1901, the most densely populated areas lay around the coalfields, sites of the Industrial Revolution (see topic 4.3). Census returns show that the proportion of people living in towns **continued** to grow from 1801 to 1901.

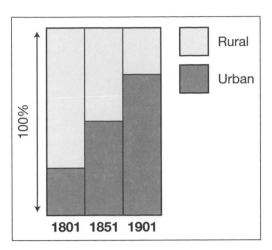

Fig. 4.1 People living in town and country – in 1801 just over a fifth of the population lived in towns, increasing to over a half by 1861.

Fig. 4.2 Population in England.

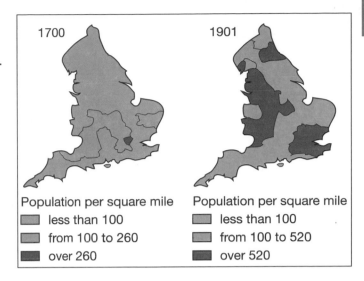

Manchester grew from 70,000 to 645,000 and Liverpool grew from 82,000 to 704,000 people in this period.

The growth figures are very striking:

1801	11.5 million
1831	17.8 million
1861	24.5 million
1901	42.1 million

Arthur Young, writing in 1774, explains that the population increase was partly due to the rise of the **birth rate**:

> *The national wealth increased the demand for labour and raised wages which led to an increase in the birth rate. … there has been an increase in employment, more marriages and, because children are not a burden, more births. As soon as a child can use its hands it can maintain itself, and the parents, too, are fully employed.*
>
> (*Political Arithmetic*, Arthur Young, 1774)

The **fall in the death rate** due to better health also helps to explain the rise of the population – shown by the graph below. Gradually, over the period, a number of factors reduced the death rate.

- **Laws** were passed by Parliament to improve people's health in terms of **housing**, **water supply** and **drainage** (see topic 4.4).

- **Food** also improved as a result of the **Agricultural Revolution** (see topic 4.2). This meant that parents could feed themselves and their own children better as each decade went by.

- **Improving technology** meant that gradually people learned how to build drains and sewers. The **materials** they needed, like iron, were plentiful enough to enable this to be done (see topic 4.3).

Key Point

Rising population in the towns was the 'driver' behind all the other changes in industry and agriculture in England in the 18th and 19th centuries.

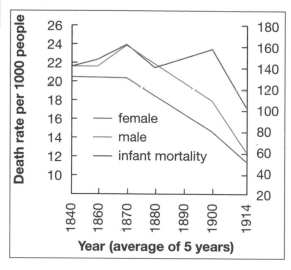

Fig. 4.3 The declining death rate, 1840–1914.

A government inspector wrote in 1800 about improved health conditions:

> *Much of the growth in population is due to better health conditions, the improvement in medical knowledge, and the improved habits among the people who are cleaner, in homes and habits, than they used to be, partly because of cheaper clothing from our cotton factories, partly because of better knowledge about running the household.*
> (Account of Persons Imprisoned for Debt in England and Wales, Arthur Neil, 1800)

The growth of Middlesborough is a good case study of the rise of urban populations during the period. The following was written by a local writer:

> *In 1831 the population was 154. In 1850 ironstone was discovered in the Cleveland Hills within reach of the Durham coal fields, making Middlesbrough an ironmaking centre. The population grew from 18,892 (1861) to 39,284 (1871) and 91,032 (1901).*
> (At the Works, Lady (Florence) Bell, 1911)

The results of rising population

The causes and effects of rising population are linked together. The most important cause was probably falling death rates.

In 21st Century Britain the birth rate has fallen so low that there is an increasing proportion of older people.

- The expanding population meant there was **rising demand for food and industrial goods**.

- This gave **incentives** to farmers and to industrial inventors and factory owners, who knew they could make money by producing goods and selling them to the growing population.

- There were **more people available to work**, so employers had more people to work for them in the farms and factories, including children (see topic 4.4). This helped more food and industrial goods to be made.

- Finally, the banks had lots of **money to lend to farmers and factory owners**. A great deal of money had come into the country from the growth of trade since the 16th century (see topic 2.6).

Progress Check

1 Where did most people live in 1700?
2 What were the two main causes of a rising population?
3 What happened to the number of people available to work in the new industries?
4 How do we know what the population was during the period?
5 Which industry grew in Middlesborough?
6 Why were people able to build drains and sewers later in the period?
7 What happened to food over the period?
8 Which two revolutions enabled all these changes to occur?

1. In the south, the south-west and East Anglia. 2. Falling death rate and rising birth rate. 3. It increased. 4. From the census. 5. Iron. 6. Better technology and materials available. 7. More was produced. 8. Industrial and Agricultural.

4.2 How and with what effects was agriculture modernised from 1750–1900?

After studying this topic you should be able to:

- explain how farms were enclosed from 1750 onwards
- understand why the old system of farming was wasteful
- identify the new methods of farming that were introduced
- understand who lost out from these changes
- list the main leaders of the Agricultural Revolution
- appreciate the links between the Industrial and Agricultural Revolutions
- explain the effects of these changes on people's living standards
- understand the variety of changes in British farming from the 1870s.

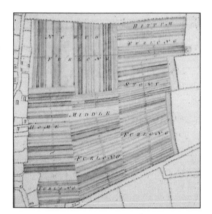

Fig. 4.4 Records of the three-field system, Strettington, Sussex.

British farmers learned how to modernise. Therefore British farmers produced enough food to feed the rising population (see topic 4.1). This is shown by the following extract from a Parliamentary debate in 1812:

> *The country should be congratulated on the growth in population and on its ability to provide the people with food.*

The way farms were organised before 1750 in most parts of Britain was **wasteful** for many reasons. One field was always **fallow** (empty). Time was wasted when tenants travelled between the **strips of land**. Animals wandered across the fields.

Enclosing the land

When land was enclosed, **fences or hedges were built** to surround the fields and farm borders. **Between 1750 and 1820** about **5 million acres** of land were enclosed, including common land and woods.

An **Enclosure Act** divided up all the land and the land-owners carved up the new farms. The General Enclosure Acts passed in 1801 made enclosure **compulsory**, enforced by the government.

Many people **suffered** from enclosure: tenants who could not prove a legal case for their tenancy got nothing. People who lived on common land or in the woods also lost out.

The following extract from a book written in 1799 explains how people suffered from the changes:

> *Time was when these commons enabled a poor man to support his family. Here he could put out his cow and pony, feed his geese and pig. Enclosures have deprived him of these advantages.*
> (*Walking Tour*, Richard Warren, 1799)

Key Point

The changes in farming created winners and losers.

New farming techniques

Many farmers gained from these changes if they used the Norfolk four course **rotation system**, which rich land-owners like Lord Townshend pioneered. Crops were rotated, so that each field grew either **wheat**, **turnips**, **barley** or **clover** in turn, all year round. Therefore no field had to be left empty (fallow), which was more efficient. The animals were provided with better feed (turnips and clover) and the soil was nourished.

Farmers also learned how to **fertilise** their land with **clay** and **lime** (marl) so that the land was able to produce more food. Animals were also heavier and healthier, so the food was also increasingly of better quality over time.

Therefore by 1900, British farming was much different from what it had been in 1750, though some areas of the country changed faster than others.

Key Point

Agricultural modernisation could not have taken place without key people investing and experimenting in new farming methods.

Key people saw the need for agricultural change, and drove the changes forwards.

Stockbreeders such as **Robert Bakewell** bred healthier and heavier animals. In 1710 the average weight of cattle sold at Smithfield meat market was 144 kg (320 lbs); in 1795 it had more than doubled to 360 kg (800 lbs).

Thomas Cooke learned how to breed heavier sheep. He educated his tenant farmers in how to fertilise the soil with marl and clover and his sheep shearing festivals were world famous.

Farmers were helped greatly by the **Industrial Revolution** (see topic 4.3), because before people learned how to produce **iron** cheaply, **farm machinery** was made of **wood**.

Changing fortunes in farming

British farmers made money selling food to the growing population and exporting it to Europe. As the Industrial Revolution continued, new **steam ploughs** and new forms of **fertilisers** made the land more profitable. The railways helped farmers sell their products more widely around the country.

Farming and industrial modernisation were linked together.

Citizenship link: Since the 1870s British farmers have been under great pressure from world competition. The rural population has fallen consistently since 1900.

However, from the 1870s, many British farmers lost out as a result of **cheap imports** of food from Canada and Argentina, as these countries were able to send their vast supplies of food on steamships, packed with wheat and freezers full of meat.

Therefore from about 1851, according to census returns, the population in rural areas started to decline, as families moved to nearby towns to look for work.

The increasing amount of food being produced and sold was a sign of rising standards of living, as working class families benefited from falling prices and increased supplies of food.

The big expansion of shops selling a wide variety of food shows that people had far more money to spend on a greater range of food in 1900 than they did in 1750.

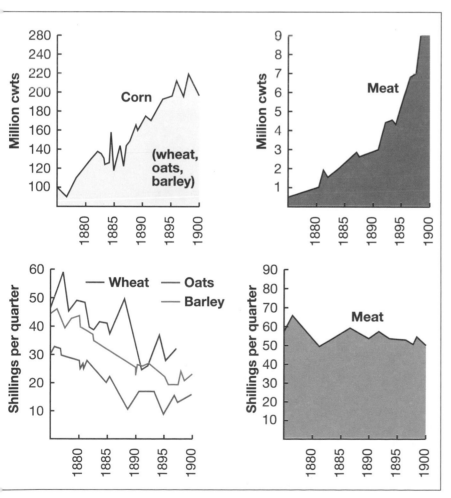

Fig. 4.5 The relationship between rising imports and falling prices.

Fig. 4.6 A well-stocked provisions store, London 1902.

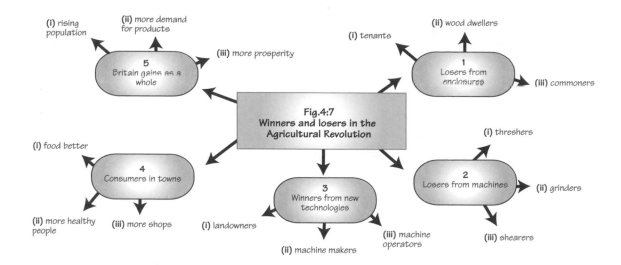

Fig.4:7
Winners and losers in the Agricultural Revolution

Progress Check

1 What was the old system of farming called?
2 What happened to the fields after 1750?
3 Name three people who modernised farming.
4 What happened to the health of the people as result of better food?
5 From what year did the rural population begin to fall?
6 When did foreign food begin to flood into Britain?

1. The three field system. 2. They were enclosed. 3. Cooke, Townshend, Bakewell. 4. It improved. 5. 1851. 6. The 1870s.

4.3 What caused the first Industrial Revolution, 1760–1830?

After studying this topic you should be able to understand:

- **what the domestic system of manufacturing was like**
- **how spinning and then weaving was mechanised**
- **the contributions of the Darby family to the Industrial Revolution**
- **the importance of the steam engine for industrial development**
- **why big factories were created for the new machines**
- **how the changes in technology were linked**
- **the effects on people of all the industrial changes.**

At the beginning of this period, everything was produced at home, so historians call it the **domestic system**. Merchants took raw materials to the cottagers and paid them for the finished work, as shown by the following extract written in 1831:

The weaver's workshop was a rural cottage from which he could go to work in his garden if he wanted. The cotton was picked clean by his young children, carded and spun by the older girls and his wife. The yarn was woven by the weaver and his sons. He took in yarn from other spinsters: one weaver could keep three spinners at work.
(*The Philosophy of Manufacturers*, Andrew Ure, 1831)

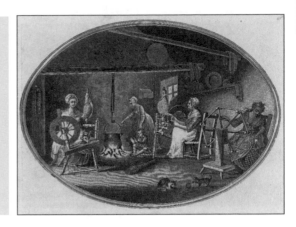

Fig. 4.8 Hand spinning in the 18th century.

Fig. 4.9 A handloom weaver.

This ancient system could not meet the **increased demand** from the rising population (see topic 4.1), so if it had continued, the people of Britain would not have had enough clothes to wear or enough fuel for their homes. Fortunately, a number of brilliant **inventors** designed **machines** to increase the amount of cloth which could be made and the amount of coal which could be dug from the ground.

New inventions in textiles

Fig. 4.10 Hargreaves' 'Spinning Jenny'.

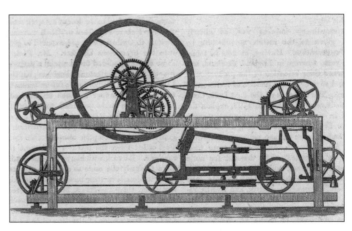

Fig. 4.11 Samuel Crompton's 'mule'.

The output of spinners was increased with the help of a series of inventions, which greatly added to the amount of **yarn** available to the weavers to make into clothes. The '**spinning Jenny**' (1764) named by **James Hargreaves** after his wife, was followed by **Arkwright's water frame** (1769) and **Crompton's 'mule'**. These machines mechanised spinning, so the old-fashioned spinners lost their jobs at home and had to go to work in the factories.

When you are learning these key people's inventions and the changes in farming, make two columns and write down the names of the inventors and the name of each innovation.

The early factories were located near rivers, because machines were powered by running water. **Lancashire** and **Derbyshire** became centres for the mills because of the damp climate which was good for the yarn, and because of the availability of rivers.

Weavers became rich because of rising demand for clothes from the growing population (topic 4.1). A writer at the time explained:

> They brought home their work in top boots and ruffled shirts, carried a cane and took a coach. They used to walk about the streets with a five pound note in their hat bands.
> (*The Life and Times of Samuel Crompton*, Gilbert French, 1860)

However, **mechanisation of weaving by 1785 ruined the weavers**, because the new steam-powered weaving loom housed in a factory could do the work of a thousand hand weavers.

Key Point

Industrial changes were caused by a combination of inventors' genius, growing demand for new products, a good climate for textile making and an abundance of raw materials like coal and iron ore.

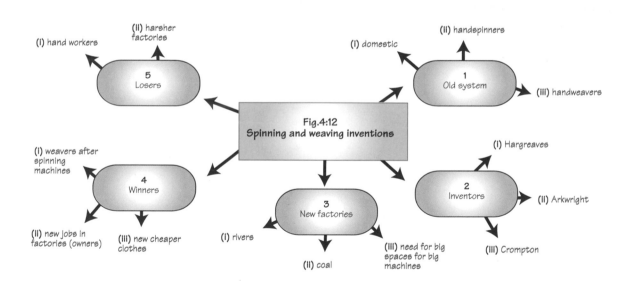

Fig.4:12
Spinning and weaving inventions

5 Losers — (I) hand workers, (II) harsher factories

1 Old system — (I) domestic, (II) handspinners, (III) handweavers

4 Winners — (I) weavers after spinning machines, (II) new jobs in factories (owners), (III) new cheaper clothes

2 Inventors — (I) Hargreaves, (II) Arkwright, (III) Crompton

3 New factories — (I) rivers, (II) coal, (III) need for big spaces for big machines

New inventions in iron

The **Darby family** from Coalbrookdale in Shropshire was the most important family of the 18th century Industrial Revolution. Abraham Darby learned in 1710 how to make **cast iron pots**, which he sold to people all over Britain and then in America. People used them for cooking and for storing food. His son, Abraham Darby II, built on his father's work in the 1740s and learned how to improve the quality of cast iron so it could be hammered into tools and machines. This was **wrought iron**. Then his son Abraham Darby III (1770s) learned how to build **bridges**, including the first Severn Bridge.

With so much iron available other inventions could be made. The **steam engine** is the most important example of a machine that could not have been made without the availability of iron. Iron production rose 1000 per cent from 1750–1830. Farmers were able to use new machines made out of iron (see topic 4.2), leading to improved food and health in the country.

Key Point

Coke was much better than coal for iron making.

The steam engine

The invention of steam engine technology was the most vital part of industrial advance.

Technological changes built on past technological change and also led to further change. The Industrial Revolution set off a chain reaction which has never stopped.

1763 James Watt improved Newcomen's engine, making it more economical and more efficient. He was financed by a Birmingham factory owner, Matthew Boulton. He was also helped by the skill of Wilkinson, who learned to make perfect cylinders while boring cannon for the armed forces.

1782 Watt, Boulton and Murdock built an engine which could drive all sorts of machines. This made **cheap mass production** possible.

Factory production

These machines used a great deal of **coal**, which increased demand. Coal production tripled from 1750–1830. The machines also massively increased the amount of clothes being made.

The effects on cotton production of the new inventions are illustrated in the following extract written by a factory owner in 1835:

We see a building with a 100 horse-power steam engine ... working 50,000 spindles ... It needs only 750 workers to produce as much yarn as would have been spun by 200,000 men.
(*History of Cotton*, Edward Baines, 1835)

Key Point

Steam power technology was the 18th century equivalent of the advanced computer today.

The factories where the clothes were made were often moved to be near the coal mines, so that steam-powered machines could be used.

At the opening of the railway in September 1830, a leading politician was killed when he got run over by the oncoming train.

Steam power was also used on the **railways** after 1825, after **George Stephenson** built the world's first passenger engine running from Stockton to Darlington, and then the Manchester to Liverpool Railway.

The Industrial Revolution generated massive **wealth** for the owners of the

Karl Marx called working class people the 'proletariat' and the factory owners, 'capitalists'.

factories, and a **new industrial middle class** was therefore created. A new **industrial working class** was also created as men, women and children worked in the new factories.

New urban centres were created. Manchester was known as 'Cottonopolis' and cotton was king. Merthyr in South Wales was the capital of iron and coal production.

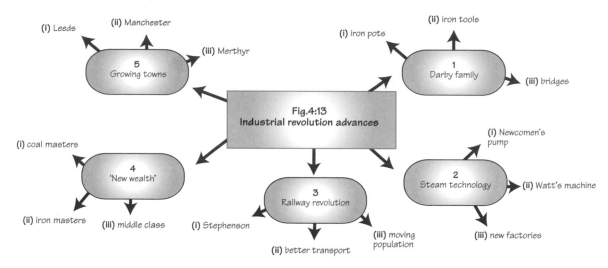

5 Growing towns
(i) Leeds
(ii) Manchester
(iii) Merthyr

Fig.4:13 Industrial revolution advances

1 Darby family
(i) iron pots
(ii) iron tools
(iii) bridges

4 'New wealth'
(i) coal masters
(ii) iron masters
(iii) middle class

3 Railway revolution
(i) Stephenson
(ii) better transport
(iii) moving population

2 Steam technology
(i) Newcomen's pump
(ii) Watt's machine
(iii) new factories

Progress Check

1 What was the name of the original factory system?
2 Which family revolutionised iron production?
3 Who invented the 'spinning Jenny'?
4 Which inventor perfected the steam engine?
5 What happened in this period to iron and coal production?
6 Name two major industrial centres of the period.
7 Who invented the first steam-powered train?
8 How was agriculture affected by the industrial changes?

1. Domestic. 2. The Darby family. 3. Hargreaves. 4. Watt. 5. There was a massive increase. 6. Manchester and Merthyr. 7. Stephenson. 8. New machines could be used.

4.4 How successful were the campaigns for factory and public health reforms in the 19th century?

After studying this topic you should be able to understand:

- why some people believed in returning to the domestic system of manufacture
- why many people opposed reform of working conditions
- why some employers and upper-class people supported reform of factory life
- how the law was gradually extended to cover more and more workers
- the state of town life in the 19th century
- how Chadwick campaigned for reform of sanitary conditions
- why progress on housing and health was slow.

Child labour

Factory owners had to force people to accept fixed times and to stay by their machines through the day. **Children** accepted much lower pay than adults so they were employed in many workplaces such as cotton mills, brickyards and coal mines.

Fig. 4.14 Children working in a brickyard, 1870.

Fig. 4.15 Children working in a coalmine.

Many employers and politicians **did not believe that it was the job of a government** to pass laws to protect workers from long hours, dangerous machinery, or even to prevent young children from working in the factories and coal mines.

Many **parents** sent their children to work to bring **extra income** into the home, so they also opposed any change in the system of child labour. **Free schooling was not provided** for everyone up to the age of 11 until **1891**, so there was nowhere for children to go if they did not go to work.

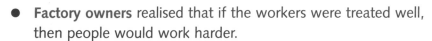

Key Point

Humanitarian responses to industrial life were very powerful, but many people tried to resist such arguments.

However, gradually many **people campaigned to get laws passed by Parliament**.

Fig. 4.16. Robert Owen.

- **Factory owners** realised that if the workers were treated well, then people would work harder.
- Upper-class 'paternalists' like **Lord Shaftesbury** led the campaign because they believed it was their religious duty to look after the poor.

In **1802 Robert Owen**, who owned a large mill in Scotland and who believed that he had a duty to look after the poor, worked with a leading Conservative politician, **Sir Robert Peel**, to get Parliament to pass an act **limiting the working day for 'pauper' children** to 12 hours.

From **1830–32 Michael Sadler** and **Ashley Cooper (later Lord Shaftesbury)** campaigned for factory reform. A Parliamentary commission heard from supporters of reform.

The extract below is a good example of evidence provided by children to investigators.

After I had worked for a half a year, I could scarcely walk. In the morning my brother and sister used to take me under each arm and run with me, a good mile, to the mill. If we were five minutes late, the overlooker would take a strap and beat us till we were black and blue. I have seen my mother weep sometimes, but she would not tell me why she was weeping.
(Joseph Hebergan's evidence to the Committee on the Factory Bill, 1832)

The factory system created great wealth and improved living standards but it also had to be made more humanitarian, since much cruelty was done to the workers in the factories.

Mary Gaskell's famous novel *Mary Barton* supported Shaftesbury. Her book condemned the factory system because it degraded women and made them neglect their children by *putting them out to nurse and letting their house go all dirty*.

In **1833** the **Factory Act** banned the employment of children under the age of nine. It also appointed inspectors to enforce its conditions.

Coal mines were awful places for children to work, as the following extract from a report of government inspectors into coal mines shows:

Children aged six or seven go down the pit at four in the morning and stay there for 11 or 23 hours a day. Their work is to open and shut the doors of the galleries when the trucks pass: for this the child sits by itself in a dark gallery for all those hours. (Report on Mines, 1842)

Children were defined as people aged 8 to 13, but 14- to 18-year-olds were not protected.

The **1842 Coal Mines Act** banned children from working underground, but brickyard work and other jobs like nail making were not banned until the 1875 Factory Act.

The **1844 Factory Act** limited children to six and a half hours work a day.

Protecting all workers

A **10-hour day campaign** led by Lord Shaftesbury forced Parliament to pass acts in **1850** and **1853**, fixing at last the working day for men and women in **textile mills** at 10 hours.

Now employers had to fence round machinery, provide eating places and toilets, and clocks to check on hours. Not until the 1875 Factory Act did workers have half days on Saturdays.

However, **agricultural workers**, **domestic servants** and **shop workers** were not protected by the law until the 1890s, because their employers were very powerful in Parliament.

Key Point

Legal protection for workers is taken for granted today, but brave people had to fight to get middle class MPs to pass these laws.

Samuel Smiles believed that workers should drag themselves up from poverty, and should not expect other people to help them.

The process of **improving working conditions** was very **slow**, as campaigners had to overcome great opposition. Even in 1900 there was very little compensation for workers if they had accidents at work, and no time off for sickness or pregnancy or even for getting married. There were no paid holidays.

The struggle for public health reform

The struggle for public health reform was also a slow and painful fight. In the new industrial towns like Manchester and Merthyr (see topic 4.3) no local government was responsible for **housing** and **sanitation**, as the following extract from a Parliamentary report in 1845 shows:

> *Merthyr is in a sad state of neglect. Because the poorer people, the majority of the population, throw all their refuse into the gutters in front of their houses, parts of the town are networks of filth.*
> (*Health of Towns Commission Report*, 1845)

The poor also had an **inadequate diet**, as the following quotation from an eyewitness indicates:

> *I visited 83 dwellings, all without furniture, old boxes for tables, stools or large stones for chairs, beds of straw, sometimes covered by torn pieces of carpet, sometimes with no covering. Food was oatmeal for breakfast; flour and water and skimmed milk for dinner; oatmeal and water again for those who had three meals a day. I saw children eating rotting vegetables in the market.* (*Tour in Manufacturing Districts of Lancashire*, William Cooke-Taylor, 1838)

Chadwick's report marks a turning point

A brave campaigner, **Edwin Chadwick**, issued a famous report which showed the appalling death rates for people in British towns. The report showed the following statistics:

Different ages of death for different classes, 1842		
The average age of death	*In Manchester*	*In Rutland*
For professional people and gentry	*38*	*52*
For tradesmen and families	*20*	*41*
For craftsmen, labourers and families	*17*	*38*
(Report on Sanitary Conditions, 1842)		

 Key Point — Chadwick's campaign was a turning point in the way governments looked after towns.

Chadwick went on to argue as follows in his report:

Careful examination of the evidence leads to these chief conclusions:

1 that the various epidemics and diseases are caused by the damp, filth and crowded dwellings in which the majority of people live;

2 that where there is drainage, street cleaning, better ventilation and other improvements, the incidence of disease drops;

3 that lack of cleanliness is due to lack of good water supplies.

(Report on Sanitary Conditions, 1842)

'Act' refers to a law passed by Parliament. A 'Bill' is a proposed law, which the House of Commons and the House of Lords must vote on. If it is approved, the monarch signs it to make an Act of Parliament.

The first Public Health Act was passed in 1848, after the water-born disease, cholera, killed thousands of people. The Act tried to make the town councils build sewers and public baths and provide clean drinking water, but this modest attempt was opposed by influential groups.

 Key Point — The new big industrial towns were very unplanned and very unhealthy and dangerous.

- **Ratepayers** did not want to pay the cost of installing sewers, drains and water supply to houses.

- **Landlords** did not want to be forced to make their houses healthy for their tenants.

- **Engineers and surveyors** were scarce in the 19th century so the task of making towns healthy was much more difficult than it was in the 20th century.

It was not until the late 1880s that most town councils took responsibility for sanitation and public health.

Although many slums were knocked down as a result of laws passed in the 1870s, very few houses were built for the poor in the 19th century. The average town dweller lived in a house that had only two rooms – one up and one down, each about 2.75 metres wide and 3.5 metres long. In such houses, families with as many as 10 children lived – without running water or toilets.

Fig. 4.17 Poor family living in a one-roomed London slum.

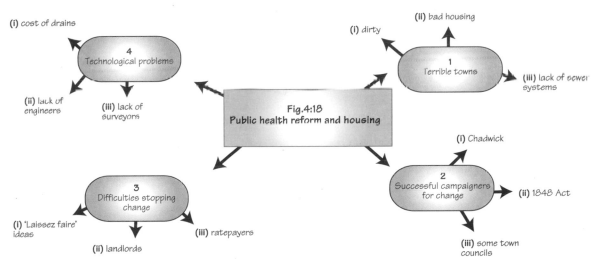

4 Technological problems
- (i) cost of drains
- (ii) lack of engineers
- (iii) lack of surveyors

1 Terrible towns
- (i) dirty
- (ii) bad housing
- (iii) lack of sewer systems

Fig.4:18 Public health reform and housing

3 Difficulties stopping change
- (i) 'Laissez faire' ideas
- (ii) landlords
- (iii) ratepayers

2 Successful campaigners for change
- (i) Chadwick
- (ii) 1848 Act
- (iii) some town councils

Progress Check

1 Who sent children to work in factories and mines?
2 Name two factory reform campaigners.
3 Name the famous Scottish mill owner who campaigned for improved conditions.
4 Who wrote an influential report on public health reform?
5 In what year was the first effective Factory Reform Act?
6 In what year was the first Public Health Act?
7 By which decade had the government passed laws to cover most factory conditions?
8 By which decade were most town councils dealing properly with sanitation?

1. Parents. 2. Sadler and Shaftesbury. 3. Owen. 4. Chadwick. 5. 1833. 6. 1848. 7. 1890s. 8. 1880s.

4.5 Why did people resort to violent protest 1750–1900 and how successful were they?

After studying this topic you should be able to:

- understand the reasons for the Captain Swing and Luddite movements
- assess how successful these protests were
- explain why there were riots in Trafalgar Square in 1887
- assess the impact of these riots.

Violent protests by the working class and clashes between rioters and the army and police were common in this period.

There was great unrest when the Napoleonic Wars ended in 1815, as the following account shows:

> *Riots broke out in London ...; at Bridport ... there were riots over the high prices of bread; at Bury by the unemployed to destroy machinery; at Newcastle by miners; ... at Preston by unemployed weavers; at Nottingham by Luddites; at Merthyr on a drop in wages; at Birmingham by the unemployed.* (*Life of a Radical*, Samuel Bamford, 1859)

 Key Point

Popular protest was caused by anger about hunger, as was the case in France in 1789 (see Chapter 3) and England in 1381 (see Chapter 1).

> Food prices were kept high by the 'Corn Laws' which stopped food from being imported.

The author of the above extract was present at the **Peterloo Massacre** in 1819, when people protested against **high food prices** and **unemployment** caused by the use of machines.

> Notice the links between events in France and England.

Handloom weavers, protesting at Peterloo, were also influenced by the French revolutionaries' ideas. The flying of the tricolour and the singing of the French revolutionary national anthem were signs that the protesters were influenced by French protesters. This fact frightened the English aristocracy who ran the government.

Fig. 4.19 The Peterloo Massacre.

The Luddites and Captain Swing

Luddites were workers who wrecked machinery in textile factories, angry that machines were taking away their jobs. They tried to destroy steam-driven shearing machines. The machine could do the work of many workers (see topic 4.2).

> Sir, ... I shall send 300 men to destroy them and we will burn down your building to ashes ... murder you and burn all your housing.
> Signed by the General of the Army of Redressers, Ned Ludd.
> (Letter sent to a Huddersfield manufacturer, 1812)

'Captain Swing' is the name given to the rioters of the 1830s. Swing men tried to destroy the property of land-owners in protest at unemployment. The following letter was sent to employers in 1830:

> Sir, Your name is among the Black Hearts in the Black Book and this is to advise you and the like of you, to make your Will. You have been the Blackguard Enemies of the People. Ye have not done as ye ought.
> Swing
> (Letter from 'Captain Swing' to a Kent farmer, 1830)

Fig. 4.20 Hay rick burning in Kent, 1830.

Why did the protestors fail?

The failure of these early protest movements may be explained by several factors:

- The protesters were campaigning against **inevitable change in technology**, which was never going to be reversed.
- The land-owners, the special constables and the army crushed them because they were **frightened** of violence turning into **revolution**.
- Almost all government and opposition MPs were against the protestors because the **MPs were mostly land-owners**.
- The **working classes had no money** to organise a proper protest movement, so they could not really challenge the authorities.
- Many **workers were doing very well** out of technological advances (see topics 4.2 and 4.3) so the majority of workers did not support the machine breakers.

Further attempts to improve the lives of workers

Between 1850 and 1870, the 'workshop of the world' provided more work for higher wages for more people. Skilled workers bought their homes, and trade unions gave them their own 'welfare state'.

Fig. 4.21 Membership certificate for the Amalgamated Society of Railway Servants.

Fig. 4.22 A 'model dwelling' for skilled workers.

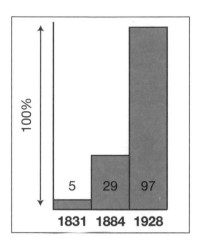

Fig. 4.23 Percentage of adults eligible to vote.

However, with the trade depression after 1870, there was **rising unemployment**. Many felt that society offered no solution to their grievances, and they demonstrated in London and elsewhere.

The following eyewitness account tells us what happened in London on 20 November 1887:

> *At three o'clock the men from the East End made towards Trafalgar Square. When the procession reached the end of St Martin's Lane the police, mounted and on foot, charged, striking in all directions. At four o'clock the procession of men from South London reached the Westminster Bridge, and the police made for them: they freely used their weapons and the people, armed with iron bars, pokers, gas-pipes and even knives, resisted.*
> (*Reynolds' News*, 20 November 1887)

Social campaigners

The riots failed to stop unemployment, but they did encourage many people to think about the conditions of poverty in which the low-paid, the sick and the unemployed were forced to live. Charles Booth visited the East End of London and reported how people lived in great poverty because of large families, old age, sickness, low wages or unemployment. Booth's brother William Booth began the Salvation Army to care for the poor of Britain's cities.

The report showed that 31 per cent of the people lived below the poverty line, fixed at an income of between 18 and 21 shillings a week. Seebohm Rowntree made his own survey of York, where he was the main employer (chocolate factories). He hoped to prove that Booth's findings did not apply outside London. To his horror he found it was the same in York.

Key Point

Rowntree and Booth were the most important social investigators in British history.

Progress Check

1 What were the Luddites protesting against?
2 Who was Captain Swing?
3 Which group of workers protested at Peterloo?
4 In what year was there a large violent protest at Trafalgar Square?
5 What law kept the price of food very high?
6 Who investigated poverty in London?
7 Who investigated poverty in York?

1. Textile machinery. 2. A rural protest leader. 3. Handloom weavers. 4. 1887. 5. The Corn Law. 6. Charles Booth. 7. Rowntree.

4.6 Why was true democracy not established in Britain by 1900?

After studying this topic you should be able to:

- identify which groups of people had the vote in 1750
- identify who obtained the vote and when
- explain why the Chartists failed to make Britain democratic by 1850
- explain why poor men also did not get the vote by 1900
- explain why women did not get the vote by 1900
- assess the effects on Britain of the extension of the franchise.

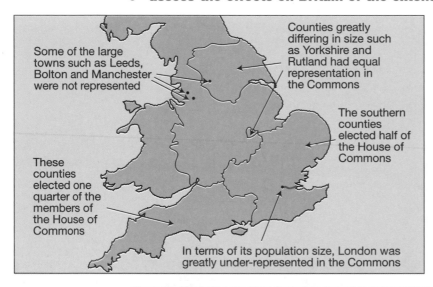

Some of the large towns such as Leeds, Bolton and Manchester were not represented

Counties greatly differing in size such as Yorkshire and Rutland had equal representation in the Commons

The southern counties elected half of the House of Commons

These counties elected one quarter of the members of the House of Commons

In terms of its population size, London was greatly under-represented in the Commons

Between 1750 and 1832, almost all the voters in Britain were rich land-owners.

Fig. 4.24
Representation in Parliament, 1830.

> **Key Point**
>
> Democracy means rule by the people, through the system of voting for the government. Democracy took a long time to be established in Britain.

As the map shows, the constituencies represented by MPs in the House of Commons were mainly in the **counties**. They were under the control of the men who owned the land.

Landlords used **threats and bribery** to make sure that people voted for the candidate they had picked to become MP. There was no secret ballot, so the landlord could see who was voting for whom.

 Rich people feared that Britain might have a revolution as the French had in 1789. See Chapter 3.

The Industrial Revolution led to the establishment of **new towns** and the creation of an **industrial middle class**, the men who owned the new factories (see topic 4.3). They were making the country rich yet **did not have the vote**. They therefore formed political unions in Birmingham, London and Manchester to campaign for more people to be given the right to vote, and for the new industrial towns to be represented.

When the **Whig Party** won the November 1830 election, they argued that a Reform Act was needed to give in to the demands of the middle class, in

In Chapter 2, you studied how Parliament became more important. The changes in the Middle Ages and in the 16th and 17th centuries affected 19th century Britain.

order to avoid revolution. In June 1832, the opponents of reform gave way and the **Great Reform Act** was passed.

The law angered many **working class** people because only one in five adult men in Britain could now vote, which was only 4 per cent of the total adult population (since no women could vote).

A charter for democracy

The **six points** of the **Charter** were:

- universal suffrage (votes for all)
- secret ballots
- payment of MPs
- equal electoral districts
- annual elections
- abolition of property qualifications for MPs.

Chartists believed that if they could force Parliament to grant the Charter, they could then get laws passed which would help the working classes.

Parliament voted by massive majorities not even to hear the petitions in 1838, 1842 and 1848. The vast majority of MPs thought that the poor had not earned the right to vote.

Fig. 4.25 Cartoon showing the Charter being presented to Lord John Russell.

Fig. 4.26 A contemporary drawing of the 1848 meeting on Kennington Common. Notice the well-dressed Chartists, the woman on the platform and a uniformed policeman (far right).

Sometimes Chartists used **violent methods** to try to force Parliament to grant the Charter, but they were easily crushed by the army and the police. In 1848, the Duke of Wellington organised the army to protect London when Chartists threatened violence, but in fact fewer Chartist supporters turned up in the rain and the movement was finished.

Chartist leaders like **Lovett**, **O'Connor** and **Attwood** were very brave and clever, but they did not have the experience or the desire to take power in the way that the French revolutionary leaders did in 1789 (see Chapter 3).

Key Point

The British ruling class was much stronger than the French ruling class at stopping revolts.

Progress towards democracy

The word democracy comes from the Greek word *demos* meaning people.

Historians now realise that the **Reform Act of 1832** opened the way to the creation of **Parliamentary democracy** in Britain.

This progress towards democracy was slow, and many people opposed it, but the following timeline summarises how Britain became a great democracy, where the people appoint and remove the government in peaceful general elections.

1867   Skilled working class men over 21 were given the vote (one third of men).

1872   All voting in elections was done in secret.

1884   Farm labourers were given the vote (two thirds of men).

1911   MPs were paid, so that working class people could become MPs.

1918   All men over 21 and all women over 30 had the vote.

1928   All women over 21 had the vote.

The effects of the **extension of the franchise** to more people were very far-reaching.

- **Political parties** had to learn how to appeal to the voters with popular policies and good leaders if they were to win elections and stay in power. The MPs had to pass laws that pleased the voters, and could not pass laws that tax-payers and rate-payers did not want to pay for.

- **Pressure groups** like trade unions and employers learned how to persuade MPs to pass laws that benefited them. Employers tried to stop trade unions becoming powerful, while trade unions tried to get Parliament to pass laws to give them legal rights.

- Working class people established the **Labour Party** in 1900 in the hope that one day a Labour government might be formed which would help the poor, as described by Charles Booth (see topic 4.5).

Key Point   Political change took a long time to achieve in Britain

Progress Check

1 When was the first Reform Act passed?
2 Which party passed this Act?
3 Which social class got the vote in 1832?
4 Which revolution had created this class?
5 What did the ruling class fear in 1832?
6 Name the political movement set up to campaign for democracy.
7 Who led this movement?
8 Who organised the British army to crush the Chartists in 1848?

1. 1832. 2. Whigs. 3. Middle class men. 4. Industrial. 5. Revolution as in France. 6. Chartism.
7. O'Connor, Lovett and Attwood. 8. The Duke of Wellington.

4.7 How much progress did women make in Victorian England?

After studying this topic you should be able to:

- understand how women's status rose in industrial England
- explain how a women's trade union movement grew
- assess the contributions to women's emancipation of leading women such as:
  - Florence Nightingale
  - Barbara Leigh Smith
  - Elizabeth Garrett Anderson
  - Millie Fawcett
  - Emily Davies.

Women who went to work in factories gained a certain amount of **independence** through earning their own wages. Female **Friendly Societies** were formed to help women save money. Women also benefited from the expansion of **state education** after 1870 as parents were prevented from sending their daughters to work until they had been to school.

Key Point
The women's movement was led by several well-off and poorer women.

In 1888 **Annie Besant** formed a **trade union of women workers** to fight for better conditions at their **Bryant and May match factory**. Besant won the support of trade unions and some newspapers. After three weeks on strike the match girls won. The strike encouraged other women to join trade unions in teaching and the civil service, where increasing numbers of women were working.

Emma Paterson, a bookbinder, founded the **Women's Protective League** for female workers, which was carried on by **Margaret Macdonald**, the wife of the Labour leader. **Isa Craig** founded the female **Association for the Promotion of Social Science**, which became a platform for the women's movement in the 1870s and onwards.

Several well-off women campaigned for women's rights across many fields, as the table on the next page shows.

Although there was still a lot to do, women were much more emancipated in 1900 than they had been in 1750. But women from all social backgrounds had to overcome obstacles from men and from many women who did not like social change.

It is work we ask, room to work, encouragement to work, an open field, with a fair day's wage for a fair day's pay – this became the professional women's motto.

Women worked hard to liberate themselves from oppression. The women mentioned here collaborated with each other to improve the status of women.

Florence Nightingale

Founded a nursing school in 1860 after running hospitals for soldiers in the Crimea War 1852–1856. This influenced **Elizabeth Blackwell**, the first English-born woman doctor, who had to qualify in the USA to lecture in medicine as women could not attend British medical schools.

Barbara Leigh Smith

Campaigned for divorce law reform and succeeded in 1857 when Parliament passed the **Marriage and Divorce Act**, which permitted women to divorce their husbands on grounds of cruelty or desertion. Won struggle for the 1881 **Married Women's Property Act**.

Elizabeth Garrett Anderson

Inspired by Dr Blackwell, became the **first practising female doctor in England** and the first woman to be elected to a School Board; got into Middlesex Hospital Training College, and then set up the all-female **Elizabeth Garrett Anderson Hospital**. By 1896 had succeeded in getting a law passed allowing women to be trained as doctors.

Millie Fawcett

Sister of Elizabeth Garrett Anderson, persuaded her husband, the Postmaster General, to allow women to work in the Post Office.

Miss Buss and Emily Davies

They both saw the need for top-class education for women. Miss Buss founded **North London Collegiate School**, inspiring Miss Beale later to take over and expand **Cheltenham Ladies College**. Emily Davies, a great friend of Dr Garrett Anderson, set up **Girton College at Cambridge University**, for women to follow degree courses.

Fig. 4.27 Florence Nightingale.

Progress Check

1 Who formed a union to help the girls at the Bryant and May match factory?
2 Which famous woman created the nursing profession for women?
3 In what year were women enabled to divorce their husbands for cruelty?
4 When were women allowed to own property?
5 Who opened up the medical profession to women?
6 Which Cambridge college for women was founded by Emily Davies?
7 Who was the first woman to be elected to a School Board?
8 Name the famous women's vote campaigner who was the sister of Garrett Anderson.

1. Annie Besant. 2. Florence Nightingale. 3. 1857. 4. 1881. 5. Elizabeth Garrett Anderson.
6. Girton College. 7. Elizabeth Garrett Anderson. 8. Millie Fawcett.

The following practice questions focus on the strand of the History National Curriculum that assesses your ability to evaluate interpretations of historical events.

1   Write a couple of paragraphs in which you explain who gained and who lost from the following historical developments. (Remember to explain why they were winners and losers.)   **[20]**
    a   The Agricultural Revolution.
    b   The Industrial Revolution.

2   Use the text and the sources to find the evidence that the Government was succeeding – or failing to help – the people under each of the seven headings. (*Hint*: Under some headings the Government was both succeeding *and* failing. Under other headings, the Government was mainly failing.)   **[20]**

Issue on which the behaviour of the government is to be judged
Looking after unemployed people and their families
Providing free schooling for young people up to 18
Protecting children at work from exploitation
Building homes for the poor and removing slums
Helping sick people to get treatment from doctors
Allowing people to vote for the government and councils
Removing the causes of poverty

5 The 20th Century World

The topics covered in this chapter are:

- Europe goes to war in 1914
- World War One on the Western Front and at sea
- World War One changes British society and European politics
- The collapse of German democracy
- World War Two 1939–45
- The Cold War 1945–90

5.1 Why did Europe go to war in August 1914?

After studying this topic you should be able to:

- understand which camps divided Europe in 1914
- describe how the Germans planned to conquer Europe
- explain why the Germans were not able to win quickly
- understand what is meant by the 'race to the sea'
- describe where soldiers dug trenches across Europe
- explain the importance to the war of the Channel ports
- assess the reasons why people welcomed war in 1914.

Key Point

World War One was fought between two blocks of countries, the armed camps of Europe.

In 1914, Europe was divided into two hostile 'armed camps'. **Germany, Austria** and **Italy** (the **Triple Alliance**) faced **France, Russia** and **Britain** (the **Triple Entente**).

Many people thought that there would not be a war because both sides had developed powerful weapons, so that no side would take a risk by attacking.

The German government drew up the famous **Schlieffen Plan** (see Fig. 5.4). The German army planned an **invasion of France**, which involved the German soldiers marching through Belgium on the way to France.

28 June 1914   The heir to the Austrian crown, Franz Ferdinand, was murdered in Sarajevo, capital of Bosnia, which the Serbs claimed was part of 'larger Serbia'. The murderer was a Serbian student called Prinzip, who was a member of the nationalist Black Hand Gang.

28 July 1914	Austria invaded Serbia, after it refused to allow Austria to send troops into Serbia to find the murderers.
29 July 1914	Russia mobilised its army, showing its wish to defend Serbia against Austria.
3 August 1914	Germany declared war on France, putting into action the Schlieffen Plan (their only plan).
4 August 1914	German soldiers marched into Belgium, following the Schlieffen Plan. Belgium was a neutral country. Britain declared war on Germany because Britain had a treaty with Belgium to protect her.
6 August 1914	Austria declared war on Russia.
12 August 1914	Britain and France declared war on Austria.

Fig. 5.1 A British view of Germany's threat to Belgium.

The **war was welcomed** by many people around Europe. There is a famous photograph of a young Adolph Hitler cheering in Vienna in August 1914, when war was announced.

In Britain millions volunteered for the army for patriotic reasons, encouraged by General Kitchener's famous recruiting poster.

A young English soldier wrote to his parents in July 1916:

> *I could not pray for a finer death, and you my dear Mother and Dad, will know that I died doing my duty to my God, my Country and my King.* (Letter from E. James Engell of the 16th London Regiment)

"YOUR COUNTRY NEEDS YOU"

Fig. 5.2 A famous – and successful – British recruiting poster.

A young recruit explained to his mother why he volunteered to fight:

> *I have no wish to remain a civilian any longer. Although the idea of war is against my conscience, I feel that in a time of national crisis like this I have no right to my ideas if they are against the best and immediate needs of the state.* (Letter from Harold Parry to his mother as he left to join the King's Royal Rifles)

A young public schoolboy explained why he volunteered to fight:

> *What really made me volunteer was less a feeling of patriotism than the wish to please my schoolmates. To have a conscientious objector at my school – even if I had wanted to be one – would have been unthinkable.* (G. Alan Thomas of the 6th Royal West Kent Regiment)

When looking at evidence, remember that propaganda is useful to historians because it tells us what the government at the time was saying.

A conscientious objector was someone who believed that war was wrong – against their conscience.

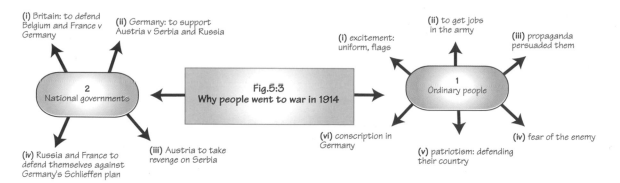

(i) Britain: to defend Belgium and France v Germany

(ii) Germany: to support Austria v Serbia and Russia

2 National governments

Fig.5:3 Why people went to war in 1914

1 Ordinary people

(i) excitement: uniform, flags

(ii) to get jobs in the army

(iii) propaganda persuaded them

(iv) Russia and France to defend themselves against Germany's Schlieffen plan

(iii) Austria to take revenge on Serbia

(vi) conscription in Germany

(v) patriotism: defending their country

(iv) fear of the enemy

Young men were allowed to join with their friends and form '**pals' battalions**'. So in many cases a whole generation in a small village went off to fight – and few returned.

Why did the German plan to quickly defeat France and Russia fail?

German plans for a quick victory on the Western Front were ruined for several reasons.

- They needed to take troops from France to fight in Russia, weakening their invading armies.
- Resistance by the British and the Belgians at Antwerp and at the Battle of Mons, August 1914, slowed down the German advance.
- German plans to take the Channel ports also failed, so the British Expeditionary Force was able to get British soldiers to the front line.

An eyewitness reported about the Mons battle:

> Remember that eyewitness accounts are useful, but they must be checked for accuracy against other accounts and also against secondary evidence.

About 100,000 British soldiers had their first taste of battle at Mons. Here the Germans faced the rapid British rifle fire. It was so fast and so accurate that the Germans thought the British had thousands of machine guns. A German wrote, 'They were well dug in and hidden. They opened a murderous fire. Our casualties increased. Our rushes became shorter. Finally the whole advance stopped, but only after bloody losses'. (The Army, P. Lane, 1978)

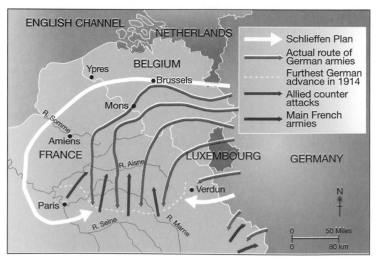

Fig. 5.4 The revised German plan, 1914, also showing the original Schlieffen Plan.

Paris was never encircled, because the Germans changed the Schlieffen Plan, after they had to take troops from northern Europe to fight Russia, whose troops had moved early. The Germans were held up by brave French resistance at the **Battle of the Marne**.

After the Battle of the Marne, both sides **raced to the sea**, to break through each other's defences, but at the first **Battle of Ypres** in November 1914 there was stalemate on the Western Front, when both sides built a huge line of **trenches** from the Belgian coast to the Swiss border with France.

By December 1914 intelligent Germans knew they could not win the war, because victory depended on Germany winning quickly.

By December 1914, the war had ceased to be a war of movement. The weather, weapons and trenches made **quick victory impossible** to achieve. **Trench warfare** became the main method of fighting for the next four years.

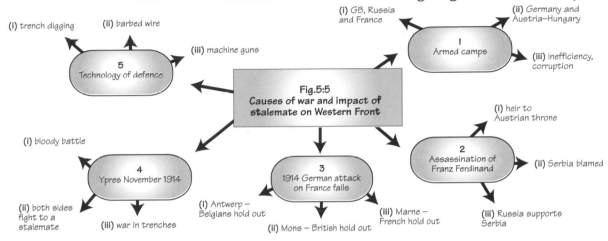

Fig.5:5 Causes of war and impact of stalemate on Western Front

1 Armed camps
- (i) GB, Russia and France
- (ii) Germany and Austria–Hungary
- (iii) inefficiency, corruption

2 Assassination of Franz Ferdinand
- (i) heir to Austrian throne
- (ii) Serbia blamed
- (iii) Russia supports Serbia

3 1914 German attack on France fails
- (i) Antwerp – Belgians hold out
- (ii) Mons – British hold out
- (iii) Marne – French hold out

4 Ypres November 1914
- (i) bloody battle
- (ii) both sides fight to a stalemate
- (iii) war in trenches

5 Technology of defence
- (i) trench digging
- (ii) barbed wire
- (iii) machine guns

Progress Check

1 Name Germany's main ally in 1914.
2 Name Britain's two main allies in 1914.
3 Which Balkan nation was allied to Russia in 1914?
4 Who was shot at Sarajevo in June 1914?
5 What was the name of the German military plan?
6 Which country did Germany invade first, prompting Britain to defend its ally?
7 At which battle in 1914 did the French hold up the Germans?

1. Austria. 2. France and Russia. 3. Serbia. 4. Franz Ferdinand, the heir to the Austrian throne. 5. Schlieffen. 6. Belgium. 7. Marne.

5.2 How was World War One fought on the Western Front and at sea?

After studying this topic you should be able to:

- describe the typical tactics for fighting
- explain how soldiers defended their positions
- understand why the generals adopted their now-criticised tactics
- appreciate the scale of casualties on the Western Front
- explain the effects of the war on Europe in the longer term
- understand how Britain won the war at sea
- explain how Britain won the war in 1918.

Trench warfare, 1914–18

After the first **Battle of Ypres** in November 1914 and the failure of either side in the war to break through the enemy lines, the men dug trenches as defensive positions, defended by barbed wire, machine guns and individual rifles. Even the best trenches became diseased and rat-infested. The rain, together with artillery bombardment which destroyed the water table, meant that drowning was a common cause of death.

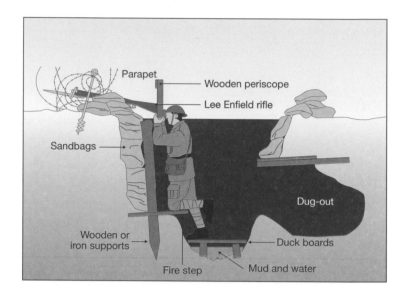

Fig. 5.6 A World War One trench.

Life in the trenches was very well described by a former soldier, Frank Richards:

> *A good trench was about six-foot deep, so that we could walk in safety from rifle-fire. In each bay of the trench we built fire-steps about two feet off the bottom. This allowed us to put our heads over the parapet. During the day we had an hour's sleep, on a wet and muddy fire-step, wet through to the skin. When anyone had to visit the company on our right he had to walk through thirty yards of waterlogged trench, chest deep in water in some places. The duckboard track was always being shelled. In some places over a hundred yards had been blown away. It was better to keep off the track, but then sometimes you had to walk through very heavy and deep mud.*
> (*Old Soldiers Never Die*, Frank Richards, 1933)

The trenches were too heavily defended to attack. For four years generals from both sides sent wave after wave of their men **'over the top'** to be killed by opposition **machine guns** and **barbed wire**. Soldiers normally had to walk because the packs they carried on their backs were very heavy.

The key moments on the Western Front in which British fought Germans

October–November 1914
The first Battle of Ypres
Germans failed to break through to the sea and to France, but they captured the Ypres 'salient'.

April–May 1915
The second Battle of Ypres
Germans tried to get through again, this time using gas for the first time. Thousands of Canadians were killed, but the British stopped the German advance.

July 1916
The Battle of the Somme
British troops ordered to try to break enemy lines. A few metres were gained.

July–November 1917
The third Battle of Ypres at Messines Ridge and Passchendaele
British tried to break through enemy lines, winning seven miles of mud.

March 1918
Luddendorf Offensive
Germans attacked and made big advances but failed to break through.

September–November 1918
British, French and American attack
Germans surrendered on 11 November 1918 at 11 am.

Huge numbers of men were killed in all the fighting. For example, at the Somme, 420,000 British lives, 195,000 French lives and 400,000 German lives were lost.

New weapons

New weapons such as the **plane** and the **tank** were beginning to be used effectively at the end of the war, but in the first three years of war the technology suited defensive tactics.

A soldier at the **Battle of the Somme**, July 1916, described what the battle was like:

For a week about 300 guns poured shells onto the Germans. The noise seemed to throb in our veins even during the quiet of the night. Then, again, in the morning, the guns opened up. For a mile, our trenches belched out dense columns of green and orange smoke. It rose, curling and twisting, blotting everything from view.

(Quoted in *The Army*, P. Lane, 1978)

Key Point War changes technology and technology changes war.

About **9 million soldiers** lost their lives in all the fighting between 1914 and 1918 – this helps to explain why most British politicians were reluctant to go to war in 1939 against Hitler's Germany.

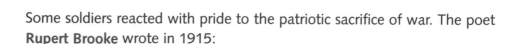

Some soldiers reacted with pride to the patriotic sacrifice of war. The poet **Rupert Brooke** wrote in 1915:

> *Now, God be thanked. Who has matched us with His hour,*
> *And caught our youth, and wakened us from sleeping*
> ('*Peace*', Rupert Brooke, 1914)

Brooke's poem was often quoted in schools and sermons.

Other soldiers were appalled at the senseless loss of life. A French officer wrote in his diary criticising the war, just before he died:

> *Mankind is mad! It must be mad to do what it is doing. What slaughter!*
> *What scenes of horror and killing! Hell cannot be so terrible.*
> *Men are mad!*
> (Lt Alfred Joubaire, quoted in *Eye-Deep in Hell*, J. Ellis, 1976)

The famous soldier poet Siegfried Sassoon attacked the way the war was fought using irony:

> '*Good morning; good morning,*' *the General said,*
> *When we met him last week on our way to the line.*
> *Now the soldiers he smiled at are most of 'em dead,*
> *And we're cursing his staff for incompetent swine.*
> ('*The Generals*', Siegfried Sassoon, 1917)
>
> *I know a simple soldier boy, who grinned at life in empty joy*
> *Slept soundly through the lonesome dark. And whistled early*
>   *with the lark.*
> *In winter trenches, cowed and glum, with crumps of lice and*
>   *lack of room,*
> *He put a bullet through his brain. No one spoke of him again.*
> ('*Suicide in the trenches*', Siegfried Sassoon, 1918)

Sometimes students get confused about bias. It is better to say that a source reveals the writer's point of view. One-sided sources are not useless since they tell us what some people thought at the time.

The war at sea

On 31 May 1916 the two fleets met at Jutland. The British claimed victory because the Germans remained trapped in port, so they could not attack Britain by sea.

Germany's ports were **blockaded**, which gradually starved the German people. Short of food, clothing, heating and other necessities, they demanded an end to the war while their troops were still in retreat, but on French soil.

The British navy had also to **protect ships** bringing goods to Britain, as the country relied heavily on imported food. Both sides used **mines** and **submarines** against the enemy.

> **Key Point**
>
> The war at sea was important because Britain's trade was by sea.

In February 1915 the Germans announced an unrestricted **submarine (U-boat) campaign** by which they threatened to sink all shipping around the British coast. This was called off in May 1916 after the USA had protested over the sinking of the passenger liner, the *Lusitania*, with the loss of American lives.

The British prime minister, Lloyd George, described German submarine warfare, 1916–18:

> *The Germans used their 'little swordfish' which had already destroyed more of our ships in a month than their cruisers had sunk during a year. Then they built many more and much larger submarines.*
>
> (*War Memoirs*, David Lloyd George, 1933–36)

> **Key Point**
>
> Lloyd George is one of the people who changed the course of history.

Because of the new convoy system, introduced by Lloyd George, the Germans lost many submarines, while a system of food rationing lessened the demand for imports.

Fig. 5.7 Cartoon showing the Germans with their 'baby', the U-boat.

The end of the war

In February 1917 the Germans announced that they were restarting the unrestricted campaign. With the **US declaration of war on Germany** (April 1917) the Allies received the benefit of fresh troops and large supplies of munitions, plus added protection for Atlantic convoys.

> **Key Point**
>
> The end of the war was hastened by the arrival of the US troops, because the Germans knew they could not defeat the American superpower.

In Germany in November 1918, the people were suffering from food shortages because of the **allied blockade**. There were anti-government risings throughout Germany. The Kaiser (monarch) fled to Holland and a new government asked for an **armistice** (ceasefire). On **11 November 1918** the war came to an end.

David Lloyd George, the Welsh-speaking Liberal prime minister, was praised in Britain as the man who won the war. Historians should note that one of his keenest supporters in the government was Winston Churchill.

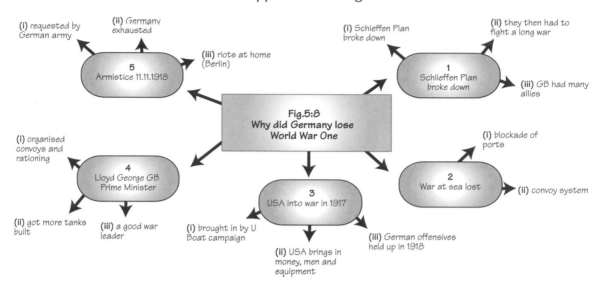

Fig.5:8
Why did Germany lose World War One

5 Armistice 11.11.1918
(i) requested by German army
(ii) Germany exhausted
(iii) riots at home (Berlin)

1 Schlieffen Plan broke down
(i) Schieffen Plan broke down
(ii) they then had to fight a long war
(iii) GB had many allies

4 Lloyd George GB Prime Minister
(i) organised convoys and rationing
(ii) got more tanks built
(iii) a good war leader

2 War at sea lost
(i) blockade of ports
(ii) convoy system

3 USA into war in 1917
(i) brought in by U Boat campaign
(ii) USA brings in money, men and equipment
(iii) German offensives held up in 1918

The effects of the war

When the war ended in November 1918, British people talked about the 'flower of England' being destroyed and that the only people who were left were 'hard faced men who had done well out of the war'. The war destroyed the monarchy in Germany and helped Adolf Hitler to come to power. The war also brought down the monarchy in Russia and helped to bring Lenin's Bolshevik Party to power in 1917.

The rise of Communism was a major cause of the 'Cold War' 1945–1990. See topic 5.6.

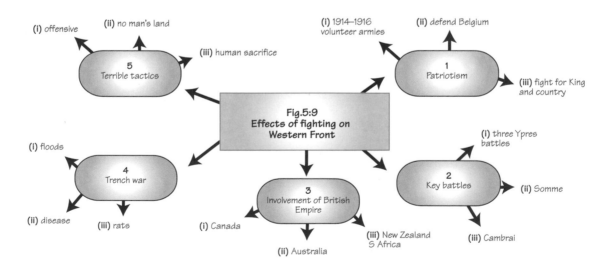

Fig.5:9
Effects of fighting on Western Front

5 Terrible tactics
(i) offensive
(ii) no man's land
(iii) human sacrifice

1 Patriotism
(i) 1914–1916 volunteer armies
(ii) defend Belgium
(iii) fight for King and country

4 Trench war
(i) floods
(ii) disease
(iii) rats

2 Key battles
(i) three Ypres battles
(ii) Somme
(iii) Cambrai

3 Involvement of British Empire
(i) Canada
(ii) Australia
(iii) New Zealand S Africa

5.3   How did World War One change British society and European politics?

After studying this topic you should be able to

- understand how the role of women was changed by the war
- appreciate how the role of governments in people's lives changed
- explain how Germany was punished by Britain and France after the war ended
- explain how the map of Europe was changed as a result of war
- understand how the way the war was ended led directly to World War Two.

The introduction of **conscription** in 1916 had never been done before in Britain. Britain's peace-time army was destroyed in 1914 and millions of volunteers died in 1915–16 (see topic 5.2), so the government had to act in a drastic fashion to keep up the effort on the Western Front. In May 1916 all unmarried men aged between 18 and 41 (and widowers with no dependants) had to sign a register making them liable for military service.

Food and diet in wartime Britain

Government **control of food supply** was another new idea for Britain. Food rationing (1918) ensured that everyone had the right to the same weekly ration of basic foods. In wartime many homes had higher incomes than in 1913 and working class people were better fed as a result.

Fig. 5.10 The opening of a communal kitchen in 1918 – food was rationed so that everyone had access to the same amount.

The wartime **improvement in working-class diet** was noted by a government report in 1919:

> From London [school medical officers] comes the report that the proportion of children in a poorly fed condition is less than half of what it was in 1913.

Key Point

War is often a big accelerator of social change.

The role of women

Votes for women came directly as a result of women working on the land and in the factories.

In 1913 Lloyd George had opposed Mrs Pankhurst and her campaign for votes for women. In 1914 she demanded the right to work: Lloyd George accepted this and millions of women joined the workforce. In 1918 a parliamentary reform Bill was amended to give women over the age of 30 the right to vote.

Fig. 5.11 'Why Women Want the Vote' – a postcard from 1909.

Key Point

World War One was the first 'total war' – everybody was involved.

An opponent of women's rights to vote described the effects of the war on the campaign for the vote:

When you are analysing sources like this, remember to apply the following tests: Who wrote it? What is in the source? For whom was it written? When and why was it written?

> Let me describe how gradually, but how inevitably we descended the slippery slope. ... An important member of the House of Commons said that it was impossible to exclude from the franchise the brave men who had fought in the war. That argument was enthusiastically welcomed, and soldiers were admitted.
>
> Then another MP said: 'If you are giving the vote to the brave soldiers, what about the brave munition workers?' ... Then a cunning MP said: 'What about the brave women munition workers?' And ... it was impossible to resist the claims of the women.
>
> (Lord Birkenhead, formerly F.E. Smith, MP, in the House of Lords, 1928)

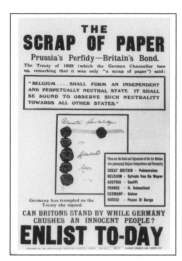

Fig. 5.12 An enlistment poster mentioned the 1839 treaty with Belgium.

Government **propaganda** was a major innovation during the war, as a way of convincing people to fight the Germans and not question the aims of the war or the tactics being used by the generals.

Music hall songs encouraged people to fight with popular verses such as:

> *We don't want to lose you. But we think you ought to go,*
>
> *For your King and your Country, Both need you so...*

Poetry that supported the war was published and read, in contrast to the anti-war poems we have seen in topic 5.2. Soldier poet Rupert Brooke's welcome for a 'patriotic' death in his poem was read out at St Paul's Cathedral:

> *If I should die, think only this of me:*
> *That there's some corner of a foreign field*
> *That is for ever England. There shall be*
> *In that rich earth a richer dust concealed*
> *A dust whom England bore, shaped, made aware,*
> *Gave, once, her flowers to love, her ways to roam,*
> *A body of England's, breathing English air,*
> *Washed by the rivers, blest by suns of home.*
> ('*The Soldier*', Rupert Brooke, 1915)

But the slaughter of the 'pals' battalions' and the conscript soldiers after 1916 changed Britain. Hundreds of thousands of children, wives and parents lost loved ones. The **war memorials** in every village in Britain reminded people of the 'blood sacrifice' of the soldiers at the front. Many surviving soldiers suffered from '**shell shock**', the term used then for mental illness caused by war. The silence on Armistice Day at 11.00 am on 11 November was always strictly observed in the years up to 1939. These horrors explain people's reluctance to fight another war and Neville Chamberlain's appeasement policies towards Hitler before 1939 (see topic 5.6).

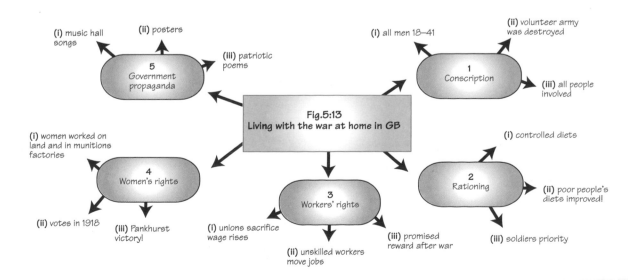

Dealing with the defeated countries

Germany was dealt with at the **Treaty of Versailles** in the famous 'Hall of Mirrors'. Mainly because of the arguments of the French leader, Clemenceau, Germany was **punished** severely regarding its **territory**, Its **defences**, its **economy** and the charge of being **guilty** for starting the war.

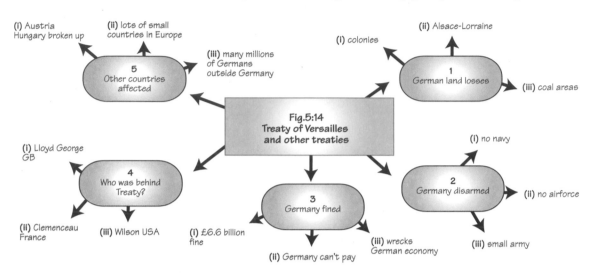

- (i) Austria Hungary broken up
- (ii) lots of small countries in Europe
- (iii) many millions of Germans outside Germany

5 Other countries affected

- (i) colonies
- (ii) Alsace-Lorraine
- (iii) coal areas

1 German land losses

Fig.5:14 Treaty of Versailles and other treaties

- (i) Lloyd George GB
- (ii) Clemenceau France
- (iii) Wilson USA

4 Who was behind Treaty?

3 Germany fined

- (i) £6.6 billion fine
- (ii) Germany can't pay
- (iii) wrecks German economy

2 Germany disarmed

- (i) no navy
- (ii) no airforce
- (iii) small army

The map below shows the changes to the boundaries of the European countries made by the Allies.

Fig. 5.15. Frontier changes in Europe after 1918.

Lost by Germany 1919	Austria-Hungary until 1918
Saar: League of Nations control 1919-1935	Plebiscite areas
Demilitarized Rhineland 1919-1936	Former territory of Imperial Russia

Most people in Britain and France wanted to punish Germany for all the horrors of war, so Lloyd George went along with the treaty, even though he knew that it was a terrible mistake to make Germany into a 'wounded lion', which would take revenge for this humiliation.

A famous English economist, John Maynard Keynes, prophesied that the Treaty of Versailles would lead to another war with Germany in 20 years. He was right, as we shall see (topic 5.3).

> **Key Point**
> The way the war was fought and ended led directly to the rise of Hitler and World War Two.

Progress Check

1 How did the government deal with the shortage of food during the war?
2 What name is given to the system of forcing people to join the army?
3 Where did women work during the war?
4 How were women rewarded for their efforts after the war?
5 Which British prime minister led the country to victory in World War One?
6 Give the precise time and date for the signing of the Armistice in 1918.
7 Name the treaty that punished Germany harshly in 1919.
8 Who was the French leader responsible for this harsh treaty?

1. Rationing. 2. Conscription. 3. On the land and in factories. 4. They were given the vote. 5. David Lloyd George. 6. 11 am on 11 November. 7. Versailles. 8. Clemenceau.

5.4 The collapse of German democracy from 1919–33

When the Kaiser fled Germany in 1918 (see topic 5.2), a new German government was formed – the **Weimar Republic**. It was begun in Weimar, a small town, as Berlin was too unstable because of riots by communists and nationalists. The new government was blamed for accepting the humiliating **Treaty of Versailles** (see topic 5.3).

The government became more unpopular as it tried to deal with the problem of **reparations** (compensation payments to the Allies). One solution seemed to be to print more money: this led to massive **inflation** (making money worth less). The price of a loaf of bread rose from two marks in 1921 to 470 billion marks in 1923. Millions of Germans saw their savings (in old marks) wiped out.

Mein Kampf was the 'Bible of Nazism'. Most people in Germany had a copy of the book before Hitler came to power in 1933.

Things became even worse in 1923. The **French army** marched into the **Ruhr** coalfields, leading to more unemployment in Germany. It was then that **Adolf Hitler** first tried to win public support. He had become leader of the **National Socialist (Nazi) Party**. In 1923 he tried to seize power by an uprising. He was defeated, tried and imprisoned. In prison he wrote his famous book, *Mein Kampf* (my struggle).

Hitler and his Nazi Party got more votes in 1932 than any other party, but they only had 33 per cent of the vote. However, the remaining 67 per cent was split among several parties, so the non-Nazi vote was ineffective.

The Wall Street Crash (October 1929) helped Hitler's Nazi Party to become the most popular party in Germany. Millions of Americans lost their jobs and savings and US banks stopped lending money to Germany – harsh times returned. With millions of Germans out of work, Hitler's Nazis became increasingly popular. Hitler promised the people of Germany that he would give them work and bread.

The senior politicians agreed to make Hitler Chancellor of Germany on 30 January 1933. They hoped they could use Hitler to get rid of unemployment and the communists, and then remove him.

The link between unemployment and the rise of the Nazis to power, 1919–33, is shown below.

	Nazi seats in the Reichstag	Communist seats in Reichstag	Unemployment in millions
May 1924	32	62	0.5
Dec 1924	14	45	0.5
1928	13	54	2.5
1930	107	77	4.0
July 1932	230	89	6.2
Nov 1932	196	120	6.0
Mar 1933	288	81	5.8

Key Point

- A combination of reasons led German democracy to fall into the hands of Hitler's National Socialist Party. National humiliation following World War One, unemployment, poverty and Hitler's personality were the main reasons.

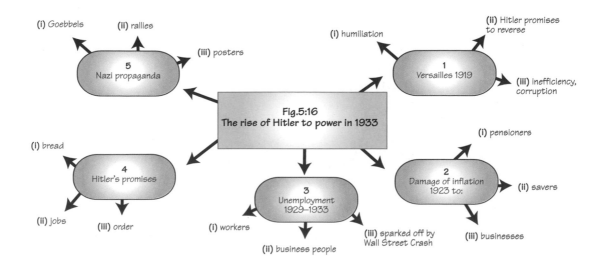

(i) Goebbels   (ii) rallies   (iii) posters

5 Nazi propaganda

(i) bread

4 Hitler's promises

(ii) jobs   (iii) order

Fig.5:16 The rise of Hitler to power in 1933

(i) workers

(ii) business people

3 Unemployment 1929–1933

(iii) sparked off by Wall Street Crash

(i) humiliation

(ii) Hitler promises to reverse

1 Versailles 1919

(iii) inefficiency, corruption

(i) pensioners

2 Damage of inflation 1923 to:

(ii) savers

(iii) businesses

Citizenship link. A totalitarian state is a state where total power is in the hands of one person or party. Can you think of countries where this is the case today?

1933–34 were the years in which Hitler made Germany a totalitarian state.

1933 Hitler was given the power of a **dictator**, following the **Reichstag fire** and persecution of all non-Nazi parties during the election campaign. In May he abolished the **trade unions** to please the employers, and in July he **banned all other political parties**, so that he had no opposition left.

1934 Hitler was made **Führer** (leader) in July 1934 and every soldier swore an oath of loyalty to him.

All these changes occurred with the support of the Catholic and Protestant **Churches**. Hitler broke his promise to leave them alone if they kept quiet about the persecution of Jews and non-Nazis.

Fig. 5.17 A Nazi rally at Nuremberg.

Joseph Goebbels ran the Nazi **propaganda** programme, with posters and rallies to convince the people that Hitler was the saviour of Germany. His use of radio and cinema was very effective, as is shown by the extract below:

February 3 1933. I talk about the start of the election campaign with the Leader. The struggle is an easy one now, since we are able to use all means of the state. Radio and press are at our disposal. The Leader is to speak in all towns having their own broadcasting stations. We transmit the broadcast to the entire people and give listeners a clear idea of all that occurs at our meetings. I will introduce the Leader's speech and I shall try to give the hearers the magical atmosphere of our huge demonstrations. (My Part in Germany's Fight, Joseph Goebbels, 1935)

Hitler's words on the use of propaganda are a very useful source for historians:

Most of the people have little intelligence, so propaganda must consist of a few points in a few simple words, repeated again and again until even the most stupid know them. In the big lies there is always a certain force of credibility. (Mein Kampf, Adolf Hitler, 1924)

Between 1933 and 1939, Hitler's policies were aimed at preparing Germany for war and also at keeping the German people's support.

Hitler did not win the majority of votes for the German Parliament in 1933. He won 44 per cent of the vote. But by 1939, there was no doubt that the vast majority of Germans welcomed his policies.

Hitler built up the army, the navy and the air force and spent massive sums on **rearmament**. The army leaders were pleased and they gave Hitler their support. Hitler needed the army on his side to stay in power. **National pride** was restored and German industrialists welcomed the profits from rearmament.

KKK stood for Kinder, Küche, Kirche – children, kitchen, church.

Workers gained from rearmament and from government-sponsored projects, such as the building of a network of motorways. **Women** were expected to breed children and be good housewives under the famous **KKK programme**.

Children were taught the Nazi version of history at school and, in their thousands, joined Nazi organisations, such as the **Hitler Youth** or the **League of German Girls**, which provided them with entertainment including holidays at summer camps.

Opponents were rounded up and put into **prison** or **concentration camps**. The **Gestapo** (secret police) hunted down enemies of the Nazis and many people betrayed their friends and work colleagues to them. Few people were willing to speak out against Hitler's policies, as a famous Lutheran pastor, Martin Niemoller, wrote:

> *First they came for the Jews. I was silent. I was not a Jew. Then they came for the communists. I was not a communist. Then they came for the trade unionists. I was not a trade unionist. Then they came for me. There was no one left to speak for me.*

He died in a concentration camp.

As well as promising to give the German people jobs and a strong country, Hitler also promised to persecute the Jewish people, whom he blamed for Germany's defeat in World War One and for unemployment.

After 1933 a step-by-step programme of **destroying the Jewish people** was begun.

1933 Many **murders** of Jewish people. Thousands were sent to Dachau **concentration camp**. Thousands left Germany as **refugees**. They fled to the USA, Britain and Palestine. Many posters were put up telling Jews they were not welcome in shops and cafés.

1935 Hitler announced a series of **anti-Jewish laws** aimed at making life almost impossible for them.

November 1938 Nazis organised a mass attack on German Jews. On '**Crystal Night**' (*Kristallnacht*) thousands

Preis 30 Pfennig
Ritualmord-Nummer
Der Stürmer
...tsches Wochenblatt zum Kampfe um die Wahrheit
HERAUSGEBER: JULIUS STREICHER
Nürnberg, im Mai 1934
Jüdischer Mordplan
gegen die nichtjüdische Menschheit aufgedeckt
Das Mördervolk
Judenopfer
Die Juden sind unser Unglück!

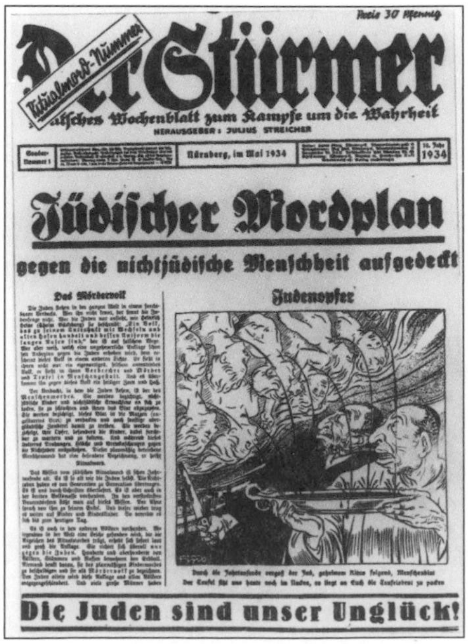

Fig. 5.18 The front page of *Der Stürmer*, a Nazi newspaper, May 1934.

Fig. 5.19 Jews are forced to scrub pavements for the amusement of the Nazis.

Fig. 5.20 A mass grave at Belsen concentration camp, 1945.

of windows were smashed in synagogues, businesses and homes and 20,000 Jews were arrested for 'resisting the forces'.

1939–45 During World War Two, Jews in German-occupied countries were sent to concentration camps, which were actually **extermination camps**.

The **Auschwitz extermination camp** is described in this extract by its commandant:

> *The 'final solution' of the Jewish question meant the complete extermination of all European Jews. I was told to set up extermination facilities at Auschwitz in June 1941. There were already three other such camps: Belsen, Treblinka and Wolzek. At Treblinka the Commandant told me that he had liquidated 80,000 in half a year, mainly from Warsaw. At Auschwitz I used Cyclon B, a crystallized prussic acid dropped into the death chamber. It took from three to 15 minutes to kill the people in the chamber: we knew they were dead when they stopped screaming. After the bodies were removed, special commandos took off the rings and extracted the gold teeth of the corpses.* (Evidence given at the Nuremburg Trials, 1947–8)

By 1945 six million Jewish men, women and children had been murdered.

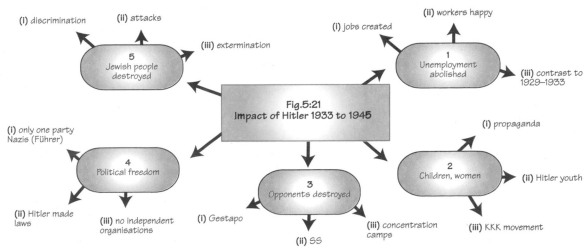

Fig.5:21 Impact of Hitler 1933 to 1945

1 Unemployment abolished
(i) jobs created
(ii) workers happy
(iii) contrast to 1929–1933

2 Children, women
(i) propaganda
(ii) Hitler youth
(iii) KKK movement

3 Opponents destroyed
(i) Gestapo
(ii) SS
(iii) concentration camps

4 Political freedom
(i) only one party Nazis (Führer)
(ii) Hitler made laws
(iii) no independent organisations

5 Jewish people destroyed
(i) discrimination
(ii) attacks
(iii) extermination

Unlike Communism in Russia, Nazism in Germany was ended by World War Two. **Hitler** committed suicide in April 1945 and his body was burned in his bunker in Berlin. Hitler's Reich was crushed by Stalin's Red Army, which was allied with the USA and Britain. Nazism fell in May 1945, when **Germany surrendered** (see topic 5.5).

Stalin died in his bed an ill man in 1953.

Progress Check

1 Which treaty was imposed on Germany in 1919?
2 What happened to money in Germany in 1923?
3 What book did Hitler write in 1923?
4 When did the Wall Street Crash take place?
5 What happened to the Nazi vote 1929-1932?
6 What was the name of Hitler's secret police?
7 Which racial group was especially targeted by the Nazis?
8 When were Hitler and the Nazis finally defeated?

1. Versailles Treaty. 2. It became worthless. 3. Mein Kampf. 4. October 1929. 5. It rose quickly. 6. Gestapo. 7. The Jewish people. 8. May 1945.

5.5 World War Two 1939–45

After studying this topic you should be able to explain:

● **why Britain declared war on Germany in 1939**
● **why Germany came close to defeating Britain in 1940**
● **the role of the USSR in the defeat of Germany**
● **how the USA helped to defeat Germany**
● **why the USA dropped the atomic bomb on Japan**
● **the effects of the war on the people of Britain and on European empires.**

Fig. 5.22 German expansion, by March 1939.

Areas taken over by Germany by March 1939

How the war occurred

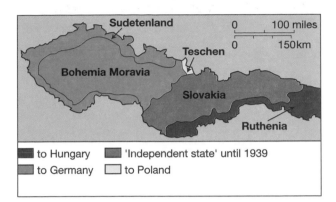

to Hungary   'Independent state' until 1939
to Germany   to Poland

Fig. 5.23 The destruction of Czechoslovakia.

Step by step, Hitler **broke the Treaty of Versailles** (see topic 5.2) and made Germany the strongest country in Europe. The British and French policy of **appeasement** allowed Hitler to get what he wanted, in an attempt to avoid the horrors of another war.

Neville Chamberlain, the British prime minister from 1935, believed that it was good to avoid war in the short term so that Britain's armed forces could be made ready.

Winston Churchill was one of the lone voices who warned that eventually Hitler would have to be defeated in war, and that if Hitler was attacked earlier rather than later, the German non-Nazis would remove him.

The following time line shows how Hitler was allowed to expand Germany's territories. Britain and France did not do anything to stop Germany breaking the Treaty of Versailles.

1933–35 Hitler ordered German factories to rebuild Germany's armed forces to prepare for war. Britain signed a naval agreement with Germany to allow Germany to build battleships.

1936 The beginning of **German invasions**. German army marched into the **Rhineland** (see Fig. 5.22). **Rearmament** accelerated and **conscription** of German men increased the size of the army. Germany also made a war alliance with Italy and Japan.

1937 Hitler tried out the new German planes by ordering them to bomb Spanish cities, including **Guernica**.

Mar 1938 German troops seized **Austria**, the land of Hitler's birth. Non-Nazis and Jews in Austria were persecuted. There was now a Greater Germany dominating Central Europe. Remember that all soldiers took a vow to follow Hitler, the *Führer*.

Sept 1938 German troops marched into German-speaking parts of Czechoslovakia (the **Sudetenland**), and this wrecked Czechoslavakia since she lost her forts and coal to Germany. The infamous **Munich Agreement** with British prime minister Neville Chamberlain, at which Chamberlain allowed Hitler to expand Germany, encouraged Hitler to become bolder.

Some people think that Britain could have defeated Hitler if the British had attacked Germany before 1939, but few people in Britain supported this action at the time.

Fig. 5.24 German police in Austria.

Mar 1939 **Prague** was bombed by the German Lüftwaffe and Germany took over the rest of **Czechoslovakia**. Neville Chamberlain was shocked and promised that Britain would stand by **Poland** if it was invaded.

Aug 1939 Hitler and Stalin organised the surprising **Nazi-Soviet Pact**. They agreed to carve up Poland.

1 Sep 1939 Hitler ordered German soldiers and the Lüftwaffe to **attack Poland**.

3 Sep 1939 **Britain and France agreed to go to war** to stop further German aggression. Hitler was shocked by Britain's decision to fight Germany. He hoped for an alliance with the British Empire, and he also thought that Britain was too cowardly to fight.

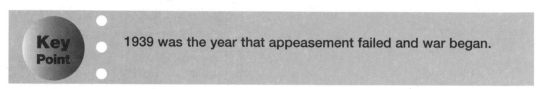

Key Point

1939 was the year that appeasement failed and war began.

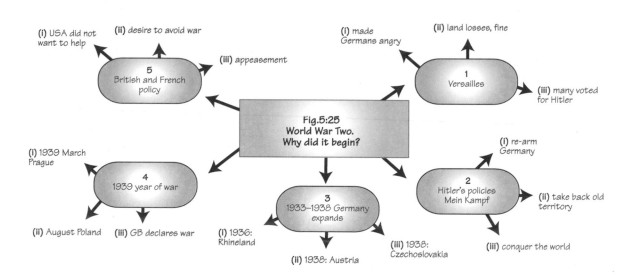

(i) USA did not want to help
(ii) desire to avoid war
(iii) appeasement

5 British and French policy

(i) made Germans angry
(ii) land losses, fine
(iii) many voted for Hitler

1 Versailles

Fig.5:25 World War Two. Why did it begin?

(i) 1939 March Prague
(ii) August Poland
(iii) GB declares war

4 1939 year of war

3 1933–1938 Germany expands

(i) 1936: Rhineland
(ii) 1938: Austria
(iii) 1938: Czechoslovakia

2 Hitler's policies Mein Kampf

(i) re-arm Germany
(ii) take back old territory
(iii) conquer the world

September 1939 to June 1940 saw Hitler's **Germany** gaining many **successes**. German conquest of her neighbours was speedy – the combined use of air force, tanks and mobile infantry in a *blitzkreig* allowed German troops to overcome less-prepared opposition.

- **Poland fell** in **September 1939**. Polish horses were no match for German planes and tanks.

- **Belgium**, **Holland** and **Norway fell** in **April and May 1940**, leading to the resignation of Neville Chamberlain to be replaced by **Winston Churchill**.

- **France surrendered in June 1940**, after British and French soldiers retreated from **Dunkirk**.

- By June 1941, Hitler's armies had smashed all of Central and Eastern Europe apart from the USSR. Only Portugal and Switzerland were not in German hands.

Key Point

Many people believe that Winston Churchill was the man who saved Britain from defeat.

The role of Winston Churchill in saving Britain and the world from Hitler is a good example of the role of the individual in influencing historical events.

Churchill encouraged the British people and the peoples of the British Empire to continue to fight Germany. The following extract is from his first speech to the House of Commons in May 1940:

I would say to this House as I said to those who had joined the government, 'I have nothing to offer but blood, toil, tears and sweat'. You ask what is our policy? It is to wage war, with all our might and with all the strength God can give us. You ask what is our aim? In one word: Victory.

Britain fought Germany alone. Hitler's plan to invade Britain, '**Operation Sea Lion**', was ordered by Hitler on 1 August 1940 and very nearly succeeded. British forces had lost many materials at Dunkirk and Germany possessed more planes and weapons than Britain.

In 1940, nobody expected Hitler to be defeated. The German defeat was brought about by six turning points.

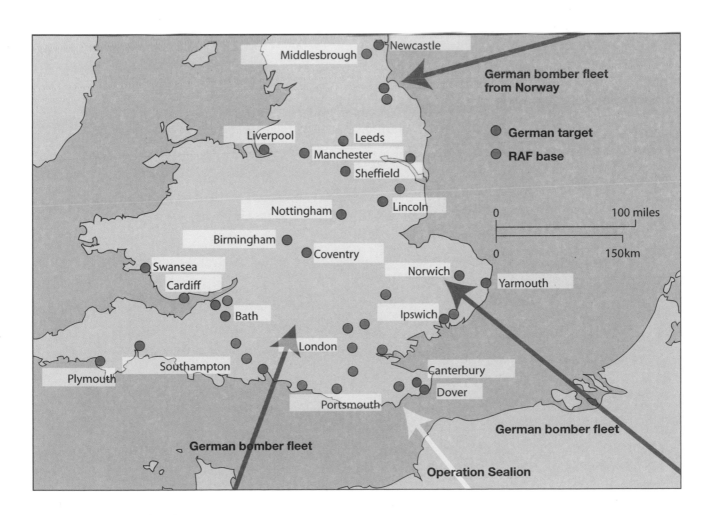

Fig. 5.26 The Battle of Britain, June–September 1940.

Key turning point 1 – the Battle of Britain, June to September 1940

Germany **failed to get control of the air** over the English Channel. The Royal Air Force Spitfire pilots just about managed to defeat the German Lüftwaffe Messerschmitt planes. Churchill said that this was Britain's *finest hour* and that *never had so much been owed by so many to so few*.

Key turning point 2 – the German invasion of the USSR

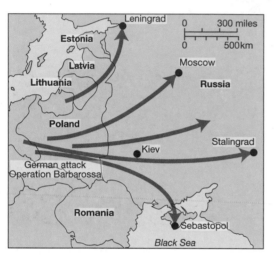

Fig. 5.27 German advances into Russia, 1941–2.

Hitler's key mistake in the war was his decision to order the invasion of the USSR in June 1941. *You only have to kick in the door and the whole rotten structure will come crashing down*, Hitler told his commanders leading the attack on the USSR.

But Hitler's decision to attack the USSR was a great mistake. **Operation Barbarossa**, as the invasion plan was known, destroyed the Germans. Here are the main reasons why the USSR defeated Hitler.

- The Russian **winter** destroyed German morale, equipment and lives.
- **Russian bravery** in the **sieges of Leningrad**, **Moscow** and **Stalingrad** stopped the Germans. Russians called their fight 'The Great Patriotic War'.
- Hitler's orders to his generals not to retreat meant that the Germans were eventually **trapped**. In January 1943, the Germans were forced to **surrender** at **Stalingrad**.
- The **huge size** of the USSR meant the country was impossible to control.
- Soviet factories produced more and more **war materials** such as tanks and planes.
- **Aid** was sent from the USA and Britain in the form of food, oil and tanks.
- The brilliant Russian general **Zhukov** organised the defence of the USSR.

Sometimes we forget that most fighting in Europe was done in the USSR. About 20 million Russians died fighting the Germans. Without their bravery, Hitler's Germany would have won the whole war.

From January 1943 to June 1944, Soviet troops drove the Germans out of the USSR. The **Red Army** then marched through **Eastern Europe**, liberating all the countries taken over by the Germans.

The **Siege of Leningrad** in 1941 was a terrible time for the people, as the following eyewitness account, written by the famous ballerina Anna Pavlova, shows:

> November 1941 arrived; icy wind drove powdered snow through the slits of dugouts and the broken windows of hospitals. The constant shortage of food, the cold weather and nervous tension wore the workers down. Few people paid any attention to the German shells that had shocked them before. In those days death loomed menacingly: lack of food and cold sent 11,000 to their graves in November.
>
> (Pavlova's eyewitness account of the siege of Leningrad, 1941)

Key turning point 3 – the USA enters the war

After Japanese planes attacked **Pearl Harbor** in the USA on December 7 1941 and Germany declared war on the USA the following day, **the Americans became powerful allies of Britain** against Germany. Britain was no longer alone.

Fig 5.28 Churchill, Roosevelt and Stalin at Yalta.

> Hitler did not need to declare war on the USA – it was a big mistake, as otherwise America may not have got so involved with the war in Europe.

The USA had more **resources** than any other country. During 1941 America's output of munitions was doubled and over 2000 aircraft produced each month. By the end of the war the USA had built 86,000 tanks, 296,000 aircraft and 140,000 ships.

Key turning point 4 – the Battle of the Atlantic, 1942–43

Germany had hoped to defeat Britain by **attacking merchant ships** carrying food, oil and raw materials to Britain. The major threat came from German submarines – **U-boats** (in 1942 more than 1100 of the 1660 German ships were U-boats). But, against all the odds, **Britain won the war at sea** because:

- British **minesweepers** were so successful that by the end of 1941, German mines were no longer a major threat.

- The threat from **British planes** forced the Germans to withdraw their warships to port.

> The Battle of the Atlantic is often forgotten, but without the Royal and Merchant Navies, the British would have starved to death during the war.

- The danger from U-boats was met by the **convoy system**: merchant ships were gathered into groups which sailed under the protection of warships and planes.

- British warships used **radar** to spot submarines which were then attacked by the ships or by planes. Over half the 750 U-boats sunk were destroyed by **air attack**.

Key turning point 5 – the Battle of El Alamein, July 1942

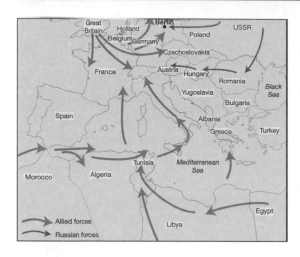

At the same time as Germany was losing in the USSR and in the Atlantic, **General Montgomery's 'Desert Rats'** halted the German advance into Egypt. From there, Allied troops pushed the Germans back and in May 1943, American and British troops pushed **Rommell's** army out of **Africa** after a series of victories in tank and air battles.

Germany was therefore being attacked from the east, from the south and, after 1944, from the west.

Fig. 5.29 The defeat of the Axis powers, 1943–45.

Key turning point 6 – D-Day

On **6 June 1944**, US, British, and Canadian troops landed on the beaches of Normandy – an event which became known as 'D-Day'. In spite of stiff resistance, they were successful with '**Operation Overlord**'.

After many losses, British and American troops commanded by General Montgomery and the US General Eisenhower **liberated France and Belgium in September 1944**.

The liberation of France, Holland and Belgium was followed by a drive to Berlin from the west, while the conquering Russians advanced from the east. On 30 April Hitler shot himself and on **8 May 1945** the **Germans surrendered. Berlin was occupied** by the Soviet Red Army and **Germany was divided** between Stalin's USSR and the western Allies.

On 'Victory in Europe Day' ('VE Day') Churchill said:

> *We may allow ourselves a brief period of rejoicing … In our long and glorious history, we have never seen a day like this.*

The defeat of Japan, August 1945

In August 1945 President Truman ordered the dropping of the first **atomic bomb** on the Japanese city of **Hiroshima**. The Americans had warned the Japanese of what was to happen if they continued to fight. This was followed by the atomic attack on **Nagasaki** and then **Japanese surrender**. Few people in 1945 opposed the use of atomic weapons against an enemy that was so cruel to prisoners and to the nations it occupied.

Truman famously said: *The buck stops here,* when talking about the awful responsibility of being American president.

Fig. 5.30 After the bomb, Hiroshima, 1945.

The Hiroshima bomb, 6 August 1945, was described by an eyewitness:

Suddenly a glaring light appeared in the sky accompanied by an unnatural tremor and a wave of suffocating heat and a wind which swept away everything in its path ... thousands in the streets scorched by the searing heat ... others screaming in agony from the pain of their burns. Everything standing upright was annihilated and the debris carried up into the air ... trams, trains ... flung like toys.
(*Warrior Without Weapon*, M. Junod)

The effect of the war on European empires

Key Point World War Two had many effects on European empires.

Before the war, many European countries held valuable colonies. The humiliation of the Europeans by the Japanese, and the self-confidence of peoples of the colonies who had fought against the invader, weakened the power of the Europeans.

The French and Dutch fought to hold on to their colonies, but finally had to abandon them. Britain withdrew from India, Burma, Ceylon and, later, Malaya and Singapore, under pressure from the people of the colonies.

It must be remembered that millions of people from the British Empire fought for Britain against Hitler's Germany. They wanted their reward to be the right to govern themselves.

Fig. 5.31 The Briitish empire.

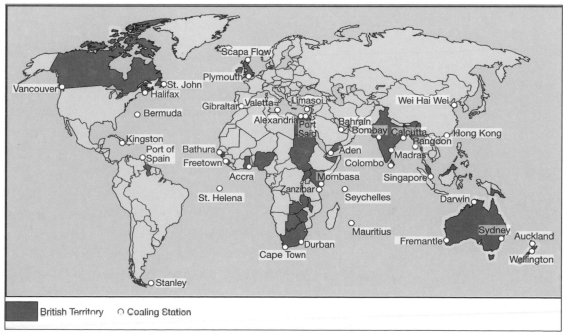

Life in wartime Britain

The government controlled the nation's economic life – industry and labour.

When the Conservative politician Winston Churchill became prime minister in May 1940 he brought **Labour politicians** into his cabinet. Men like **Attlee** (deputy prime minister) and **Bevin** got the credit for winning the war alongside Churchill.

Fig. 5.32 London children were evacuated to the safety of the countryside.

Fig. 5.33 A London street 3 minutes after an air attack.

Well-off people in safer suburbs took in evacuated children from bombed cities. The poverty and ill health of the children from industrial Britain shocked some middle class people who had not met poor people before.

On 5 July 1945, while still at war with Japan, Britain held a general election. Soldiers serving overseas voted and sent their voting papers home. This meant that the result was not known until 26 July.

Churchill's Conservative Party lost in a most surprising result. The Labour Party, led by **Clement Attlee**, won their first majority. Many well-off people voted Labour for the first time as a result of meeting poor people on the battlefield and at home.

The war **helped the Labour Party** to come to power because the people, having won the war, now wanted to **win the peace** and have a **National Health Service**, **new houses** and proper **social security**. They felt they deserved these rewards for defeating the Germans, and that the Labour Party would provide them. It did so, between 1945 and 1951.

Stalin, leader of the USSR, genuinely could not understand why Churchill would allow there to be an election and why he would allow himself to lose! In the USSR Stalin ordered the murders of millions of opponents.

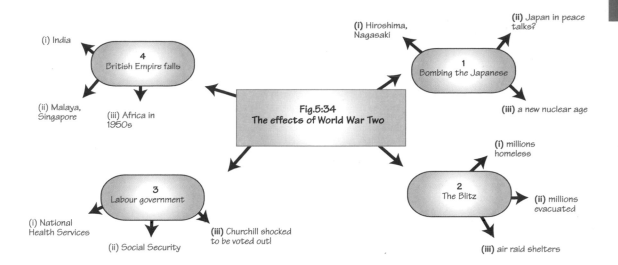

Fig.5:34
The effects of World War Two

- 4 British Empire falls
  - (i) India
  - (ii) Malaya, Singapore
  - (iii) Africa in 1950s
- 1 Bombing the Japanese
  - (i) Hiroshima, Nagasaki
  - (ii) Japan in peace talks?
  - (iii) a new nuclear age
- 3 Labour government
  - (i) National Health Services
  - (ii) Social Security
  - (iii) Churchill shocked to be voted out!
- 2 The Blitz
  - (i) millions homeless
  - (ii) millions evacuated
  - (iii) air raid shelters

Progress Check

1 In what year did World War Two begin?
2 Who led Britain from 1940–45?
3 Who led the USA during the war?
4 Who led the USSR during the war?
5 What were the six turning points in the war?
6 How did the peoples of the British Empire react to the war?
7 Which political party won power in Britain after the war?

1. 1939. 2. Churchill. 3. Roosevelt and Truman. 4. Stalin. 5. Battle of Britain; War in USSR; USA enters the war; Battle of the Atlantic; Battle of El Alamein; Normandy landings. 6. They wanted self-rule. 7. The Labour Party.

5.6 The Cold War, 1945–90

After studying this topic you should be able to understand:

- **how Europe divided into two enemy camps from 1945–48**
- **why the United Nations was established**
- **how the Cold War affected the peoples of Europe**
- **how the Cold War affected people outside Europe**
- **why the Cold War came to an end in 1989–90.**

The end of World War Two

Churchill and **Roosevelt** met in Casablanca in January 1943 and announced that the war would go on until Hitler and his allies had 'surrendered without conditions'.

Stalin took over USSR in 1922 and ruled it until 1953 when he died.

Stalin met with them in Teheran in November 1943 and discussed the future of post-war Europe. That discussion continued when the three met at **Yalta** in **February 1945** and **Potsdam** in **July 1945**.

They agreed to **divide Germany** between the allied powers, each having a 'zone'. They agreed that the liberated countries would be free to choose the kind of government they wanted. Poland took land in eastern Germany and the USSR took eastern Poland. The United Nations was set up to avoid war.

The birth of the United Nations

The first meeting of the 51 member nations of the United Nations (UN) took place in January 1946. They agreed to set up the following structures to keep the nations of the world at peace. In the words of Churchill, *Jaw, jaw is better than war, war!*

The General Assembly supervises the work of several important agencies, such as the UN International Children's Emergency Fund (**UNICEF**). Other agencies are linked to the UN, including the **World Health Organisation (WHO)** and the **United Nations Refugee Organisation**, which was set up to look after the millions of refugees fleeing Stalin's regime and seeking a better life.

The Secretariat, under the Secretary-General, runs the UN's day-to-day affairs.

In 1948 the UN produced the Universal Declaration of Human Rights.

Citizenship link: Rights and duties of the citizen are very important.

Extract from the Universal Declaration of Human Rights

Everyone has the right to work, to free choice of employment, protections against unemployment.

Everyone has the right to equal pay for equal work.

Everyone has the right to remuneration ensuring for himself and family an existence worthy of human dignity...

Everyone has the right to leisure and holidays with pay.

Everyone has the right to a standard of living adequate for the health of himself and his family ... food, clothing, housing and medical care and the right to security in unemployment, sickness, widowhood, old age ...

Everyone has the right to education ... free ... compulsory.

Education shall be directed to the full development of the human personality ... respect for human rights and freedoms ... tolerance among nations, racial or religious groups...

Key Point

However, the world was not as perfect as the writers of the Charter hoped.

The iron curtain divides East from West

Fig. 5.35 Russian control of Eastern Europe, 1944–47.

Stalin's army liberated the countries of Eastern Europe, but he imposed communist governments on **Poland**, **Bulgaria**, **Hungary**, **Romania**, **Czechoslovakia** and **Yugoslavia**. Winston Churchill said that an **iron curtain** had come down over Europe from the Baltic to the Adriatic. Behind this line, Stalin's USSR controlled the peoples of Eastern Europe by means of the secret police, murders of political opponents and enforcement of a **one-party (communist) state**.

Germany was divided into **four zones**, occupied by the USA, Britain, France and the USSR. Berlin, deep in Eastern Germany, was also divided into four zones, run by the same 'Big Four' nations.

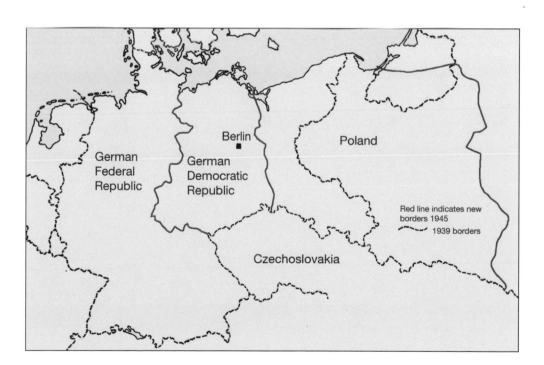

Fig. 5.36 The division of Germany and enlargement of Poland.

Stalin argued that Russia had been attacked in 1914 and 1941 through Eastern Europe when its governments had been hostile. He wanted to make sure that, in future, governments there would be friendly. Stalin and many people in the USSR were also suspicious of western capitalism. In the West, people were suspicious of Russian communism.

The 'Truman Doctrine' was the basis of US policy until 1990 and the fall of communism in Eastern Europe.

The new US president, **Harry Truman**, explained his **anti-communist doctrine** to Congress in 1947:

> *At the present moment every nation must choose between alternative ways of life. One way of life is based upon the will of the majority. The second is based on the will of a minority imposed on the majority.*

Stalin's government killed about 30 million of its own people 1922–1953.

The United States poured billions of dollars into Europe after 1948, to save Europe from starvation and from Stalin's USSR. This aid programme was known as the **Marshall Plan**, after the American politician General George C. Marshall.

In April 1949 **NATO** (the North Atlantic Treaty Organisation) was set up to protect the world from communism. The USSR retaliated in 1955 with the **Warsaw Pact**, bringing together all the communist countries of Eastern Europe. These two organisations became two opposing armed camps, building more and more nuclear weapons, which were very dangerous and costly. This period of threatened conflict was known as the **Cold War**.

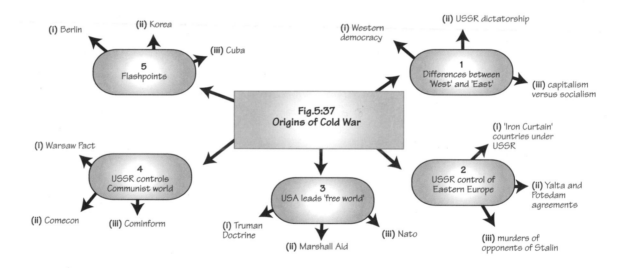

Fig.5:37 Origins of Cold War

East versus West in the Cold War

During the Cold War (1948–1990), both the communist world led by the USSR and the capitalist world, led by the USA were often on the verge of nuclear war. Both the USSR and the USA fought each other 'by proxy'.

The table on the next page itemises some of the key events in the Cold War period.

y dates in Cold War	Actions by Communist nations	Actions by Western nations	Who came out on top?
ne 1948–May 1949 rlin blockade crisis	Blockade of West Berlin to starve West Berliners. Roads and rail links with the West were cut.	Airlifts of supplies of food and other vital materials by British, US and French planes, risking pilots' lives.	USSR lifted the blockade after 11 months. They failed to break West Berlin, led by Mayor Reuters.
61 rlin Wall Crisis	Khrushchev, the Soviet leader after Stalin's death, ordered a wall to be built around West Berlin to stop people leaving East Germany for the West. The guards shot people who tried to escape.	US president John F Kennedy visited Berlin and told the people *I am a Berliner*, vowing to protect people's freedom.	The wall remained until November 1989, when it was destroyed by the people of Berlin at the end of the Cold War.
ctober 1962 e Cuban Missile Crisis	Khrushchev tried to land nuclear missiles on Cuba, not far from the US coast, and threatening most US cities with long-range missiles.	President Kennedy forced the USSR to back down and remove the missiles, and the USA promised not to invade Cuba.	Kennedy became a hero of the 'free world' but he was assassinated in 1963. A telephone hot line between the USSR and USA was set up to try to avoid war.
56 and 1968 ngarian and echoslovakian crises	Khrushchev sent armed forces into Budapest (Hungary), and later, Soviet president Brezhnev sent armed forces into Prague (Czechoslovakia) to stop the people there breaking away from communism. The USSR wanted to warn other 'iron curtain' peoples, such as the Poles, not to revolt.	The USA, Britain and the 'free world' protested but could do nothing. They did not wish to start a nuclear war with the USSR. The West decided to increase their nuclear weapons to defend themselves.	In the short term, the USSR won, because it stopped anti-communist protests. Many protesters were sent to prison in the USSR.
45–90 e nuclear arms race the 1980s both armed mps had enough eapons to destroy each her several times over utually assured estruction)	After Hiroshima, the USSR built thousands of nuclear missiles which could be launched from land or by submarine. Space rocket technology was used. The USSR had far more 'conventional' forces. The Soviets found they could not use their nuclear weapons in their failed invasion of Afghanistan.	At the same time the USA and her allies built a similar number of nuclear missiles, which could also be launched from land or sea. Many people in the West protested against nuclear weapons. The USA found that nuclear weapons did not stop them losing the Vietnam War (1963–75).	The nuclear arms race between the Warsaw Pact and NATO was brought to an end when President Gorbachev (USSR) called for an end to communism. In 1987 all long–range missiles were eliminated.
958–2003 e European Union (EU)	The ex-communist countries of Eastern Europe applied to join the EU.	They were accepted into the EU in 2003 (joining date: May 2004).	The European Union became an ever stronger union of people in terms of wealth and politics.

The Cold War ended in 1990–91 when President Gorbachev allowed free elections in the USSR, and the other nations of Eastern Europe quickly adopted democracy. Communists were driven from power.

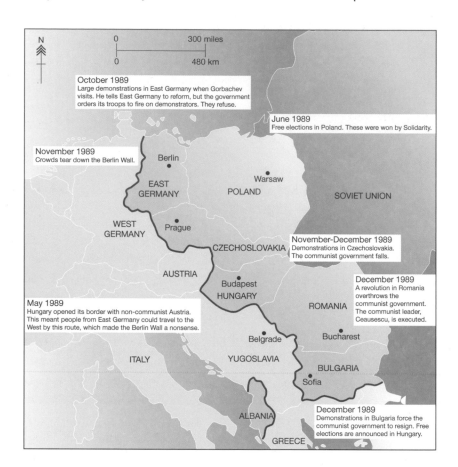

Fig. 5.38 Key events leading to the end of the Cold War.

Text on map:

October 1989 Large demonstrations in East Germany when Gorbachev visits. He tells East Germany to reform, but the government orders its troops to fire on demonstrators. They refuse.

June 1989 Free elections in Poland. These were won by Solidarity.

November 1989 Crowds tear down the Berlin Wall.

November–December 1989 Demonstrations in Czechoslovakia. The communist government falls.

December 1989 A revolution in Romania overthrows the communist government. The communist leader, Ceausescu, is executed.

May 1989 Hungary opened its border with non-communist Austria. This meant people from East Germany could travel to the West by this route, which made the Berlin Wall a nonsense.

December 1989 Demonstrations in Bulgaria force the communist government to resign. Free elections are announced in Hungary.

Key Point

During the Cold War there were many conflicts but the USSR and USA never came to all-out war against each other.

Progress Check

1 In which two cities did Britain, the USA and the USSR discuss the shape of Europe in 1945?
2 Which American general organised massive aid to Europe after the war?
3 Which international organisation was set up in 1945 to try to keep world peace?
4 Which German city was divided between the USSR and the western allies?
5 Name the two eastern capital cities invaded by the USSR in 1956 and 1968.
6 Over which central American country did the USA and USSR come close to war in 1962?
7 Which Soviet president brought an end to the Cold War?
8 In which year are the ex-communist countries of Eastern Europe to enter the European Union?

1. Yalta and Potsdam. 2. Marshall. 3. The United Nations. 4. Berlin. 5. Budapest and Prague. 6. Cuba. 7. Gorbachev. 8. 2004.

The following practice questions focus on the strand of the History National Curriculum that assesses your ability to evaluate interpretations of historical events.

1   Analysing the causes of World War.   **[10]**

a   Do you agree that Germany alone was guilty for starting the First World War?
Give reasons for your answer. Refer in your answer to the role of Serbia, Austria, France, Britain and Russia.

b   In your view, what was the single most important cause of the war starting in 1914? Give reasons for your answer. Show how the cause you have selected is linked to the other factors.

2   Reflecting on the effects of the war on the soldiers and people at home.

When the war finished, most people in Europe and in the USA said that the war should not happen again. Using the text and the extracts in Chapter 5.2, produce newspaper articles about the war.

a   In the first article explain why the war was so terrible that it should never again be fought.   **[10]**

b   In the second article, explain why the war was still necessary.   **[10]**

c   In the third article explain the advantages and disadvantages of the way in which Germany was treated after the war ended.   **[10]**

d   Using the evidence in the text and sources in chapter 5.3 explain how many people benefited from the war.   **[10]**

3   Analysing the reasons for Germany's defeat in World War Two.
Germany was finally defeated in May 1945 for a combination of reasons.
These include: **[20]**

i   Germany's failure to win the 'Battle of Britain'.
ii   Germany's failure to defeat the USSR.
iii   The entry into war by the USA after the bombing of Pearl Harbor.
iv   Germany's defeat in the Battle of the Atlantic.
v   British victory at El Alamein.
vi   Winston Churchill's leadership.
vii   The attacks on Germany after D Day in 1944.
viii The bravery of British generals and soldiers.

Write a paragraph on how each of these factors influenced the result of the war.
Are any of these factors connected to each other?
Do you agree that Germany's war with the USSR was the most important reason for Germany's defeat? Explain your answer.

4   The Cold War 1945-1990
Do you agree that the Western Allies were more to blame for the problems of the Cold War than the USSR and its allies? Give reasons for your answer, by weighing up the contributions made by each armed camp and concluding with which side was most to blame.
You could conclude that both sides were to blame for the Cold War.   **[20]**

6 The black peoples of the Americas

6.1 How was the slave trade organised and how did it affect black people?

After studying this topic you should be able to:

- understand how the 'triangular' trade system worked
- explain why many people supported slavery
- show how Britain got rich out of the slave trade
- understand what life was like on the slave ships
- appreciate how slavery affected black people in America and the West Indies.

The triangle of trade

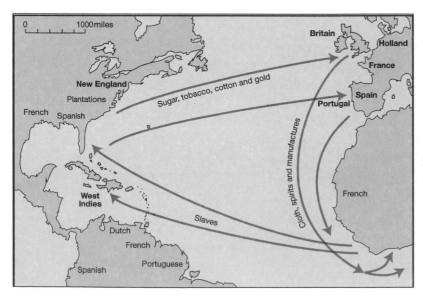

The slave trade was part of the 'triangle of trade' between Europe, Africa and the Americas. Britain took a full part in that trade triangle, competing with the other European nations like France and Belgium.

The slave trade triangle is the starting point for the slave trade question.

Fig. 6.1 The triangle of trade.

On **side 1** of the triangle, ships left Bristol, Liverpool, London and other ports, carrying cotton and metal goods made in Britain. When the ships reached Africa, traders bought men, women and children from African chiefs. Many Africans were snatched by gangs of men employed by a 'slaver'.

On **side 2** of the triangle the slaves were carried to the colonies to be sold to the owners of plantations. This was known as the middle passage. The slaves were kept in chains below decks in filthy conditions for the 100-day journey to the West Indies or the Americas. Many died on the way while others were simply thrown overboard while still alive so that slave traders could claim for their loss through insurance policies.

MPs heard the following account from someone who went on a middle passage voyage:

> She had taken in 336 males and 226 females on the coast of Africa. After she had been out seventeen days she had thrown overboard 55. … But the thing that struck us most forcibly was how was it possible for such a number of people to live, packed as tight as they could cram in low cells, three feet high, without light or air, with the temperature at 89 degrees.   (Evidence to Committee on Slave Trade, 1791)

Slaves who survived the journey were sold at the slave markets that operated in the ports of the West Indies and the Americas. People who wished to buy slaves were told of the auction by notices in newspapers and by handbills. At a slave auction, the bewildered Africans were bought and sold just as, in a modern market, people buy and sell cattle or sheep. The slaves worked on plantations growing sugar, tobacco or cotton.

Some African slaves came to Britain to be servants of rich people here.

Many became domestic servants: cooks, cleaners, drivers or children's playmates.

By 1780 over 300,000 slaves were being carried every year in Liverpool-owned ships alone. Slavery in the United States grew fast after 1793. As the number of cotton plantations grew, so did the demand for slaves. When importing of slaves was banned in 1808, southern states bred their own slaves. By 1861 there were 4 million slaves born in the USA.

On **side 3** of the triangle of trade, the ships carried sugar, rum, tobacco, raw cotton, timber and other goods for sale in Britain and Europe. English cotton mills, especially in Lancashire, used the raw cotton (see Chapter 3).

Fig. 6.2 Slaves were white people's property, traded in open market and families were split up to suit the buyers.

Who benefited from the slave trade?

Many people benefited from this triangular trade, in which slavery was vital.

- **Industrialists** and **workers** gained. In 1770 one third of Britain's cotton goods went to Africa to be exchanged for slaves, while half went to the colonies to provide clothing for the slaves.

- **Slave-ship owners** made vast profits from the sale of slaves. Many ships carried over 700 slaves per trip and made the owner over £5000 a voyage.

- **Banks** and **industry** as a whole benefited from the cash generated by slave trading.

- **Ports** connected with the slave trade prospered. London saw the building of many new and large docks specifically built to cater for the colonial trade: West India Docks (1802), London Docks (1805) and East India Dock (1806).

 Key Point — Many, many people had vested interests in the slave trade and many ordinary people supported it.

Life as a slave

The American slave's day was very harsh, as the following extract from a diary shows:

5.30 a.m. *To the field carrying breakfast with them; register called; work until 8.00.*
8.00 a.m. *Breakfast of boiled yam, edoes, okra. Latecomers are whipped.*
8.30 a.m.–12.00 noon *Work.*
12.00–2.00 p.m. *Dinner of salted meat or pickled fish. Rest.*
2.00–6.00 p.m. *Work.*
6.00 p.m. *Return to huts.*

(Plantation Work, 1807)

Fig. 6.3 Treadmills like this were introduced to the West Indies as an 'improved' form of punishment.

In the vast majority of cases, **life for slaves was extremely miserable**. Slaves were harshly punished by cruel overseers. Families were split up when they were sold at auction, and the father, mother and children were sent to different parts of the West Indies or America.

African-American music was a response to this oppression. The famous songs called 'spirituals' spoke of freedom, heaven and bearing the trials of life. The black American leader W.E.DuBois called them *sorrow songs*. He said the songs *tell of death and suffering* but that *Through all the sorrow of the songs there breathes a hope – a faith in the ultimate justice of things*.

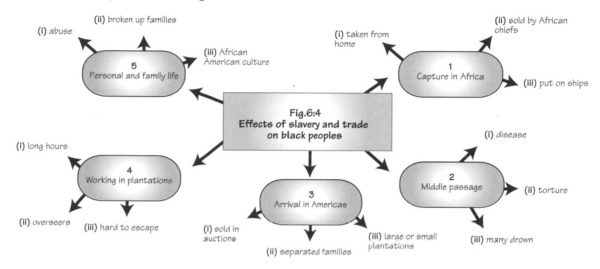

Fig.6:4
Effects of slavery and trade on black peoples

- 1 Capture in Africa
  - (i) taken from home
  - (ii) sold by African chiefs
  - (iii) put on ships
- 2 Middle passage
  - (i) disease
  - (ii) torture
  - (iii) many drown
- 3 Arrival in Americas
  - (i) sold in auctions
  - (ii) separated families
  - (iii) large or small plantations
- 4 Working in plantations
  - (i) long hours
  - (ii) overseers
  - (iii) hard to escape
- 5 Personal and family life
  - (i) abuse
  - (ii) broken up families
  - (iii) African American culture

Progress Check

1 What was the name of the second side of the trade triangle?
2 To which countries did captured African people get sent?
3 Who sold the African people to the slave owners?
4 Which products were grown on slave plantations?
5 Name some English ports that did well out of slavery.
6 Which product was brought to English mills in Lancashire?
7 What happened to the families of those who were enslaved?

1. The middle passage. 2. The West Indies and America. 3. African chiefs. 4. Tobacco, sugar and cotton. 5. Bristol, London. 6. Raw cotton. 7 They were split up.

6.2 How easily was the institution of slavery abolished in the British Empire?

After studying this topic you should be able to:

- describe the key turning points in the struggle to abolish the slave trade
- describe the key people in the abolition of the slave trade
- explain why some people wanted to abolish the slave trade
- explain why many people wanted to keep the slave trade
- understand how eventually slavery was abolished in the British Empire.

> **Key Point**
>
> The process of abolishing slavery was slow and painful. Firstly, Parliament was persuaded to abolish the trade in slaves. Then, when people got used to this, they were prepared to abolish slavery completely and free the slaves.

A legal decision of 1729 showed that a slave was his master's property. This is shown by the following legal case extract:

> *We are of the opinion that a slave by coming from the West Indies to Great Britain, either with or without his master, does not become free, and that his master's property in him is not in any way changed.*
> (Decision by Yorke and Talbot, Crown law officers, 14 January 1729)

This decision was challenged in 1765–67 by **Granville Sharp** (1735–1813), a leading Church man. In 1765 he met a former slave, Jonathan Strong, who had been beaten by his master and become a runaway. Sharp nursed him and found him work. In 1767 Strong's master saw him, and had him captured and put on board ship for Barbados. Sharp took the case to court, where the Lord Mayor of London ruled that Strong should be freed.

Sharp was also involved in the notorious case of the **slave ship Zong**, which had left Africa in 1781 with 440 slaves. During the journey many died, and 133 sick slaves were thrown overboard. The owners of the Zong claimed the insurance money for 'lost cargo'. Sharp helped the insurance company in its refusal to pay, and in the ensuing court case.

'Quakers' are normally called 'The Society of Friends'.

In 1787 Quakers persuaded an evangelical MP, William Wilberforce, to act as the Parliamentary spokesman for the Abolition Committee. Wilberforce brought several Bills for abolition before Parliament from 1789 onwards. It was not until 1807 that Parliament finally agreed to **abolish the slave trade** throughout the Empire.

Traders, merchants, industrialists and ordinary people who looked down on black people were opposed to the abolition of slavery.

Slave traders were given £20 million in **compensation** for the loss of their property. This was a huge amount of money – in the same year the government gave £20,000 to schools in Britain.

In 1808 the USA followed Britain's example and abolished the trade in slaves, although slave breeding continued in the southern states of America. In 1815 European governments outlawed the slave trade.

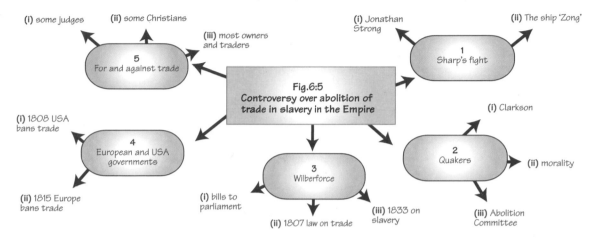

(i) some judges (ii) some Christians (iii) most owners and traders

5 For and against trade

(i) 1808 USA bans trade

4 European and USA governments

(ii) 1815 Europe bans trade

Fig.6:5 Controversy over abolition of trade in slavery in the Empire

3 Wilberforce

(i) bills to parliament
(ii) 1807 law on trade
(iii) 1833 on slavery

(i) Jonathan Strong (ii) The ship 'Zong'

1 Sharp's fight

(i) Clarkson

2 Quakers (ii) morality

(iii) Abolition Committee

After the slave trade was abolished, people then campaigned for the abolition of slavery itself. Huge meetings were held to publicise the cause. Anti-slavery pamphlets were written and petitions were presented to Parliament, where, after Wilberforce became ill in 1824, the abolitionist case was led by Thomas Fowell Buxton. Between 1807 and 1830, the Abolitionists had little success for many reasons.

Many people believed that slavery was good for the Africans, as is shown in this speech:

> *I oppose immediate emancipation because it would exchange the evils now affecting the negro for others which are more serious … bloodshed and war.* (W.E. Gladstone, Newark, 1832)

People who ran the British Empire thought that the slaves were unfit to be free:

Remember: one-sided sources are useful to historians writing about the past. We learn what people thought at the time, why they thought as they did, and how things changed.

> *Henry Taylor (of the Colonial Office) said that he was well aware of the consequences of emancipation both to the negroes and the planters. The estates of the latter would not be cultivated; it would be impossible, for want of labour; the negroes would not work … they wanted to be free merely that they might be idle.* (Memoirs, Charles Greville, 1852)

The end of slavery

Key Point

In the end, economic factors and fears of slave rebellions led to slavery being abolished.

Cuba and Brazil began to produce cheaper sugar, so that West Indian plantations were closed down. The successful revolt by slaves on the French island of St Dominique and the island's winning of its independence (1804), made West Indian slaves restless. In 1831 Jamaican slaves rose in revolt and 100 were shot and 300 hanged once the rebellion was put down.

Parliament decided to abolish slavery in the British Empire so as to avoid further uprisings. On 1 August 1834 slavery was finally banned by Act of Parliament. Wilberforce was on his death bed.

- All slaves under the age of six years were to be freed immediately.
- Slave owners were to receive about £337.50 for each slave they 'lost'.

Progress Check

1 Name the main leader of the campaign to abolish slavery.
2 Which religious group played a big role in the campaign to abolish slavery?
3 In which part of the world did British people own many slaves?
4 What did anti-abolitionists think would happen to the freed slaves?
5 When was the slave trade banned by the British Parliament?
6 When was slavery itself abolished by the British Parliament?

1. William Wilberforce. 2. Quakers. 3. The West Indies. 4. They would become lazy and revert to 'barbarism'. 5. 1807. 6. 1834.

6.3 How was slavery in the United States of America eventually abolished?

After studying this topic you should be able to:

- **understand why America was divided over the issue of slavery**
- **describe who led the fight for the abolition of slavery**
- **explain why many people still supported slavery**
- **understand the role played by Abraham Lincoln in the abolition of slavery**
- **explain how the American Civil War began in 1861**
- **appreciate the importance of the 13th Amendment of the US constitution.**

Abolitionists in America

Key Point Many kinds of both black and white people became Abolitionists in the United States.

- **William Lloyd Garrison** used his newspaper, *The Liberator*, to fight against slavery.

- **Sojourner Truth** was a runaway slave and became a great religious speaker at Abolitionist meetings.

- **Charles Sumner** was a white senator who was attacked for making a stirring speech against slavery.

- **John Brown** led a raid on a weapons store to arm the slaves but he was captured and arrested.

- **Frederick Douglass** bought himself out of slavery, taught himself to read and write and was the main leader of the black people of America in the 1850s.

- **Harriet Beecher** wrote a famous novel, *Uncle Tom's Cabin*, in 1852. The book described the cruel nature of slavery. Some 300,000 copies were sold and it made a deep impression on people.

Arguments in favour of slavery

Slave owners said slaves were essential to the future of the tobacco, sugar and cotton plantations. Slaves were cheap to employ and they could be controlled much more than free workers.

Fig. 6.6 A white 'overseer' and black cottonfield workers.

Southerners feared a slave rebellion, like the one led by **Nat Turner** in 1831, when 55 whites were killed. They welcomed the fugitive slave laws against runaway slaves. They also welcomed the ruling by the courts in 1857 that a slave was *his master's property* and that *no law can take away the master's right to that property*.

Civil war breaks out

Abraham Lincoln was elected president in November 1860 and took office in March 1861. Southerners feared that they would have to abolish slavery in their states and that any new states that were formed could not have slavery. Therefore, by April 1861, **eleven southern states broke away from the United States** and created a Confederate Army. They elected **Jefferson Davis** as their president.

Key Point
- Lincoln is considered by some to be one of the most important people in the history of the world. He was the founder of the modern United States and the man who freed the black Americans from slavery.

Fig. 6.7 The American Civil War divided the country, south against north.

Victory for the 'free' north

After the north won its first major victory, Lincoln proclaimed that slavery was going to be abolished. **The Emancipation Proclamation**, 1 January 1863, is a very famous historical source:

> *All persons held as slaves within any State, or part of a State, the people of which shall be in rebellion against the United States, shall be then, and forever, free.*

The **13th Amendment** to the American constitution (1865) outlawed slavery, and every southern state had to accept this Amendment if they wanted to rejoin the United States of America.

It was another two years before the south finally surrendered (9 April 1865), when Lincoln expressed his hopes for a peaceful and united country in another very famous speech:

> *With malice towards none, with charity for all, with firmness in the right as God gives us to see the right, let us strive on to finish the work we are in; to bind up the nation's wounds – to do all which may achieve a just and lasting peace among ourselves.*
> (Second inaugural address)

Fig. 6.8 Abraham Lincoln.

Lincoln's murder on 14 April 1865 was a cruel 'reward' for winning the Civil War and abolishing slavery.

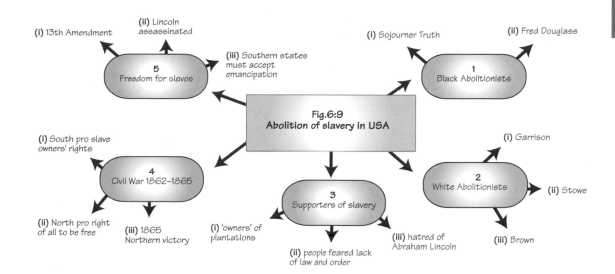

Fig.6:9
Abolition of slavery in USA

5 Freedom for slaves
(i) 13th Amendment
(ii) Lincoln assassinated
(iii) Southern states must accept emancipation

1 Black Abolitionists
(i) Sojourner Truth
(ii) Fred Douglass

4 Civil War 1862–1865
(i) South pro slave owners' rights
(ii) North pro right of all to be free
(iii) 1865 Northern victory

3 Supporters of slavery
(i) 'owners' of plantations
(ii) people feared lack of law and order
(iii) hatred of Abraham Lincoln

2 White Abolitionists
(i) Garrison
(ii) Stowe
(iii) Brown

Progress Check

1 Which US president abolished slavery in the USA?
2 States in which part of the country supported slavery?
3 Who wrote Uncle Tom's Cabin?
4 What was the main product of the southern slave plantations?
5 By what Amendment was slavery abolished?

1. Abraham Lincoln. 2. The south. 3. Harriet Beecher Stowe. 4. Cotton 5. 13th.

6.4 How did the USA make the change from slavery to freedom in practice?

After studying this topic you should be able to:

● understand how the government tried to bring freedom to the former black slaves
● explain how white people took away that freedom
● explain why most southern white people hated the new laws of freedom
● explain how the courts stopped African Americans becoming truly free
● understand how many African Americans tried to change their circumstances
● explain when freedom began to be won for African Americans.

Helping former slaves

After the Civil War was won by the northern Federal Armies, the USA passed a series of laws.

The **14th Amendment** to the US constitution (1868) provided equal protection under the law for all people in the USA. The **15th Amendment** (1870) gave the vote to black people.

The government set up the Freedmen's Bureau, to help the former slaves and poor whites, which:

- provided aid (including food) to the many whites and blacks who otherwise would have starved

- set up over 100 hospitals and over 4000 schools to educate black children.

Fig. 6.10 School teachers came from the north ('Yankee schoolmarms') once it was legal for blacks to learn to read and write.

Racism continues

The **Ku Klux Klan (KKK)** was a white terrorist group. It terrorised, shot and lynched black people. Many KKK men were poor whites, angered by African American freedoms. For a time government troops protected black people from the KKK, but in 1877, the government withdrew the army from the south. Black people were again left to the mercy of the KKK.

Fig. 6.11 The Ku Klux Klan used racial hatred as a political weapon.

Key Point

It took a long time for many white Americans to see black people as free and equal.

After 1877, in the south, votes were given only to those who 'qualified'. Literacy tests, ownership tests and 'grandfather' clauses were designed to stop the freed slaves being able to vote. KKK gangsters and the police used force to keep blacks from voting. The result was that, in Louisiana, for example, between 1896 and 1904 about 129,000 blacks out of 130,000 lost the right to vote.

Some ex-slaves became **sharecroppers**, giving part of their produce for the rent of a plot of land owned by a white landlord. Some hoped to improve their lives by moving to the 'freer' north.

In the south, the white governments followed the example of South Carolina, which was the first to bring in **'Jim Crow' laws**. These denied blacks equal rights almost everywhere – black people were not allowed to eat in 'whites only' hotels or restaurants; they could not sit in 'whites only' seats on buses and trains; their children were denied entry to 'whites only' schools, colleges and universities.

> These events show us that real change is often very slow. Attitudes take a long time to change.

Even in the 1930s African Americans were often physically attacked, with their attackers rarely being arrested or punished. Thousands of blacks were arrested and many of them were lynched by white mobs, usually led by Klansmen with the support of seemingly 'decent' white people. The African American Frederick Douglass said that former slaves were *left free from the master* but were *slaves of society*.

Fig. 6.12 A lynching in the 1930s.

The black civil rights campaign

There was similar **discrimination and violence in the north**. In July 1919 a black boy, swimming in Lake Michigan, drifted over to waters reserved for whites. He was stoned from the white beach and drowned, which led to a week-long series of race riots in Chicago in which 40 people died.

Some African American people had the courage to campaign for the advancement of black people.

The former slave, **Booker T. Washington**, founded a college in Alabama and urged blacks to become qualified so that they might have better job prospects.

W.E.B. Dubois had been educated at the elite Harvard University. He helped set up the **National Association for the Advancement of Colored People** (NAACP) which campaigned for equal treatment for black Americans.

Garvey is one of the founders of Rastafarianism.

Marcus Garvey founded the Universal Negro Improvement Association. Garvey disagreed with the NAACP's desire for black people to integrate with white people. He argued that African Americans should separate themselves from white people, improve themselves and become a *black nation*.

> **Key Point**
>
> The 'Road to Freedom' was still far away for black Americans when World War Two broke out in 1939.

President Roosevelt had refused to pass a law to ban lynching. There was still **segregation** in the armed forces and in public places. Many southern states still banned black people from voting.

Read Chapter 4 on how voting rights were given to all people in Britain by 1918.

During the 1950s black people **organised protests** against the fact that they were being segregated in schools and public places. They also protested more and more against laws which stopped them from **voting** in elections. In 1954, the US Supreme Court banned segregation in schools, but many white people refused to obey the law and in the southern states of America segregation continued until the late 1960s.

It was not until the 1960s when black Americans like **Martin Luther King** and **Stokely Carmichael** joined forces with Presidents Kennedy and Johnson that African Americans began to win real freedom and the right to vote.

Today, General Colin Powell and Condeleza Rice are African American senior members of the US government.

In the **Mexico Olympics** in 1968, three black American athletes made the '**Black Power**' salute to publicise the fact that black people were still being treated as second class citizens. The greatest boxer in the world got rid of his 'slave name' Cassius Clay and took on a Muslim name, **Muhammad Ali**, to show that slavery still had to be overcome.

This famous protest song inspired black people to fight for greater freedom and equality of opportunity:

> *We shall overcome, we shall overcome,*
> *We shall overcome some day.*
> *Oh, deep in my heart, I do believe,*
> *That we shall overcome some day.*

Fig. 6.13
Martin Luther King.

Martin Luther King delivered his famous '*I have a dream*' speech on 28 August 1963 at the Lincoln Memorial in Washington. His speech to hundreds of thousands of people inspired millions of Americans. Many of his sentences began with the famous line: *I have a dream*.

... that one day this nation will rise up and live out the true meaning of its creed – we hold these truths to be self evident:
that all men are created equal ...
that ... the sons of former slaves and the sons of former slave owners will one day be able to sit down together at a table of brotherhood ...
that my four little children will live in a nation where they will not be judged by the colour of their skin but by the content of their character.

His speech finished with the famous rallying call:
Free at last! Thank God Almighty, we are free at last.

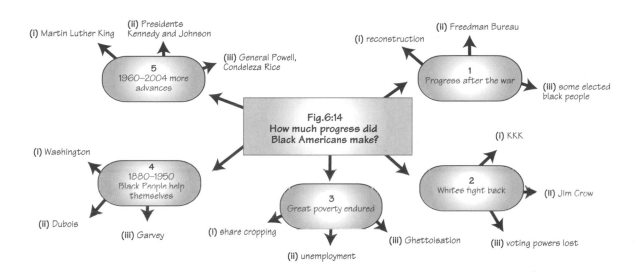

Fig.6:14
How much progress did Black Americans make?

5 1960–2004 more advances
(i) Martin Luther King
(ii) Presidents Kennedy and Johnson
(iii) General Powell, Condeleza Rice

1 Progress after the war
(i) reconstruction
(ii) Freedman Bureau
(iii) some elected black people

4 1880–1950 Black People help themselves
(i) Washington
(ii) Dubois
(iii) Garvey

3 Great poverty endured
(i) share cropping
(ii) unemployment
(iii) Ghettoisation

2 Whites fight back
(i) KKK
(ii) Jim Crow
(iii) voting powers lost

Key Point

Racism as a way of thinking is still a long way from being eradicated.

Progress Check

1 Which Amendment to the US constitution gave black people the right to vote?
2 Which Amendment gave black people equal treatment under the law?
3 What was a share cropper?
4 What was the name of the white terror gang?
5 Which laws discriminated against black people?
6 Name three campaigners for the advancement of black people.
7 In which decade did African Americans make significant progress in terms of equality?

1. 14th Amendment. 2. 15th Amendment. 3. They farmed plots of land and gave produce to the landowner as rent. 4. The Ku Klux Klan. 5. Jim Crow laws. 6. Washington, Garvey, Dubois. 7. 1960s.

The following practice questions focus on demonstrating your ability to investigate historical questions on your own, using the evidence from the text and the sources.

Research task
Produce a project on the slavery of the black peoples of the Americas.
You should try to cover the following areas listed below.

1   The organisation of the slave trade and its effect on black people   [10]

a   How was the slave trade triangle organised?
b   Who benefited from the slave trade?
c   What was life like on the 'middle passage' for the enslaved people of Africa?
d   What was life like for slaves in the American plantations?

2   The abolition of slavery in the British Empire   [10]

a   What arguments did people use to support and oppose the slave trade?
b   Why was slavery eventually abolished within the British Empire?

3   The abolition of slavery in the USA   [10]

a   Why was it so difficult to abolish slavery in the United States of America?
b   How did many black and white people campaign to abolish slavery?

4   The change in the USA from slavery to freedom   [10]

a   What problems did the black peoples of America suffer after they had won their freedom?
b   What steps did African American people take to improve their own lives?

Answers

Answers here are given in note form. Please refer back to the relevant sections to check your answers more fully.

Chapter 1

1 King Harold's claims:
   - Edward the Confessor chose him, the Saxon Earls elected him.

   Hardrada's claims:
   - King Harthacnut promised the throne to him.

   William's claims:
   - Edward the Confessor and Harold Godwinson had promised him the throne.

2 You should answer the question in five separate paragraphs referring to the following points.

   i The feudal system gave control of the land to William who ruled the country in alliance with the barons and knights. Everyone had to obey their superior. At the top of the tree was the KIng.

   ii Castles dominated the surounding villages. English people were forced to obey the baron in the castle. Castles were difficult to attack and easy to defend until gunpowder was invented.

   iii Oath of Salisbury reinforced the idea of obeying the King who was also supported by the Church. An oath was a special religious promise and it was difficult to break that promise. If a person broke the oath they were killed by the King's men!

   iv The crushing of rebellions by the English and Normans showed that William was never going to be removed as King. In the middle ages, weak Kings failed to crush rebellions and this led to civil wars.

   v The Domesday Book showed that William was a very efficient ruler. He knew his new kingdom was rich and the people knew that William had good knowledge about all the property of England.

3 Key Points you should mention:

   Reasons for building castles: control of the country by the King and the Barons. Symbols of power.

   Methods of Defence: building on hills, moat, drawbridge, throwing tar, firing arrows.

   Methods of Attack: laying siege, mining, arrow attacks, cannons, climbing towers.

   Developments: early castles were wood, later castles were stone buildings of keeps and round towers.

4 Key Points you should mention:

   a Training as a page: to serve, to ride, to wear armour. Squires hunted and accompanied the knight. Vigil to prepare for knighthood.

b Knights' duties were not easy: service and chivalry.

c People became knights for excitement, money, prestige, because the boy's family expected it.

5 Key Points you should mention:

Life was very hard for the ordinary family. High rents had to be paid to the Lord. Farming the strips of land.

Sowing, ploughing, harvesting, repairing their huts. Black Death killed one third of the people and wiped out whole villages: it was a terrible curse on the people, but wages rose after the Black Death.

6 Your spidergram should mention:

Bishops controlled the Diocese in which people lived. Their Church was the Cathedral. They controlled the priests and the people. Monasteries were homes for nuns and monks. These people were meant to be holy, to pray, to care for the sick and the poor and to study. Priests looked after the people; were the only educated people. Church life was based on mass and a centre for social activity. Lollards, led by Wycliffe, wanted changes in the church.

7 Craftsmen were trained workers who made the goods. Wool merchants sold wool from farms to towns and abroad. Wool villages were wealthy and Kings taxed them. Shop keepers sold goods made by craftsmen. Streets were named after the types of craft and shops there. Villagers travelled to town to buy and sell.

8 Peasants were angry with high rents and feudal dues and the Lord. Ex-soldiers wanted higher wages.

Religious Protesters wanted more equality in England. Taxpayers hated the poll tax. Ball and Tyler were the main leaders.

9 Similarities: English use powerful armies, build castles, ally with people in Wales and Scotland. English divide and rule Wales and Scotland.

Differences: Welsh were easier to conquer. Scotland was further away from London, the land was harsher to overcome, the Scots had brilliant fighting leaders.

10 Magna Carta was a contract between the King and the Barons. King needed their consent to tax and to make laws. Simon de Montfort forced the King to call Parliaments; organised elections to Parliament.

King Edward 1 agreed to calling parliaments together in order to raise taxes in return for actions to please the Members of Parliament. The King was not a total dictator.

Chapter 2

A 1 Anne Boleyn. **2** Martin Luther. **3** Mary Queen of Scots.
4 Oliver Cromwell. **5** Mary Tudor. **6** Simon de Montfort.

B 1 The right of kings to make the law – God had appointed them – no questioning of King.

2 Spanish Armada sent to invade England – defeated by Drake and Howard – triumph for Elizabeth.

3 Parliament elected House of Commons. MPs grew in importance, had to agree to pay taxes, be consulted by the King and pass laws, agreed to remove Charles 1.

4 The Act of Supremacy made Henry VIII the Head of the new Church of England. Everyone had to sign an oath to accept the new power of the King. Thomas More and John Fisher refused to do this and so were executed.

5 Europe to Africa to America; cotton, gold, slaves, made England rich.

C 1 Use all documents, A – C: brutal, clever, Protestant, beginning of democracy, supreme ruler.

2 Find examples of Source B backing up Source A, and contradicting Source A; mainly backing it up.

3 Source C: Cromwell had too much ambition; B defends Cromwell; authors of sources are on opposite sides.

D Use as much detail as possible from topics 2.3 to 2.6. Do not forget the conclusion on her strengths/weaknesses. Main topics: Religion, Armada, Mary Queen of Scots, her personality, trade and living standards.

Chapter 3

A 1 Revolution is transfer of power

2 corruption, taxes, poverty

3 soldiers spread ideas of change

4 starvation and anger of people

5 more say in running of France

6 the nobles did not pay; the poor paid most

7 clergy, nobles, peasants

8 Liberty, Equality, Fraternity, Republicanism

B 1 and 2 No right or wrong answers. Be ready to explain your answers.

3 Each factor caused unpopularity of the King's Government to grow. Government unable to deal with the problems, which made the opposition grow even more! Revolution had many causes, not just one cause.

4 King's mistakes prevented him from closing the divisions and solving food shortages. His foreign wars added to problems and the anger of the people. The riots in Paris and the National Assembly actions were results of failure of the King, but remember these problems were building up over many years.

C Use different colours for the six branches of the diagram. Use the text to put some details on the diagram, such as under the victims of the Revolution the names of people killed. Benefits include: ending of feudalism, rule of law, the right to vote. Impact on Europe: events in Britain and Ireland; symbols of revolt.

Chapter 4

1 a Winners from Agricultural Revolution: Landowners, Farmers, Consumers. Losers: Commoners, Woodland dwellers, Hand workers.

b Winners from Industrial Revolution: Factory owners, Inventors, Skilled workers, People with higher living standards; Losers: Hand workers, Workers with cruel bosses, Child labourers, Workers suffering accidents.

See the text to show why these people did well or badly. Basically the people in Britain who could meet the demand for their labour did well. People who were weak or did not meet the demand suffered.

2 By 1900 the role of Government had slowly grown from 1750, but there were many gaps.

Unemployed people and their families had no help. Charities like the Salvation Army provided food, but many died from hunger, disease and the cold.

Free Schooling by 1900 only extended to children age 12. All other schooling was fee paying, so only rich people went to school.

Protection at Work had been achieved by several Factory Acts controlling ages, hours, condition.

Homes for the Poor. By 1900 the Government had made a start in clearing slums and building houses, but not many areas had actually seen this happening. Most poor people lived in appalling conditions.

Sick people received no Government help with doctors' fees or hospital fees. High death rates from sickness and pregnancy.

Voting rights. Poorer men and all women were excluded from voting for MPs, but women ratepayers voted for local councils and school boards.

The real causes of poverty were not solved by the government. It was up to each individual to look after themselves. Old age, sickness, unemployment, child birth, death of parents were the main causes.

Chapter 5

1 a Causes of World War One. Serbians assassinated Franz Ferdinand. Austria attacked Serbia. Russia attacked Austria, Germany defended Austria and attacked France via Belgium, bringing Britain into war. Germany was main cause but not only cause of the war.

b Think about whether the Schlieffen Plan was the single most important reason; bringing all the countries into the war. Germany put the plan into practice. Trouble in Serbia sparked off the war.

2 a Terrors of war: Trenches, Offensives, Death rate, Futility of war, Propaganda, more wars caused by war.

b Need for war: Defend Belgium, Patriotism, stop rise of Germany. Honour.

c Advantages: punished Germany, justice, rewarded France and Britain, tried to stop Germany attacking again.

Disadvantages: Germany wants revenge, rise of Hitler, weak states in middle of Europe.

d Benefits of war: higher living standards, more jobs, women's role grows, voting rights, Government helps people more during the war.

3 USSR's role in war started defeat of Germany; loss of men, arms, morale. Germany retreats from the East 1943–45. Was most important reason. Battle of Britain and Atlantic protected the air and sea routes. Pearl Harbor brings USA into war – weapons, money, men, morale. El Alamein good for GB morale, bad for Germany, Germany retreats from Africa. Churchill held country and free world together: speeches. D Day began the end of the war, but 'ordinary' soldiers and generals like 'Monty' must not be forgotten.

4 Cold War. Western Allies and USSR allies contributed. Suspicions, histories of attacks, different systems, leaders, the nuclear arms race all contributed. By 1990 the West had won and 'capitalist freedom' spread.

Chapter 6

See the text and sources in Chapter 6.

For each of the 4 questions, try to write about 150 words. Use bullet points and spider diagrams if you wish.

Self-assessment

General levels of response marking schemes will help you to assess the level at which you are working when you answer the practice questions.

Take responsibility for your own learning, by seeing what sort of response you are giving to the practice questions at the end of each chapter.

Level descriptions for history at Key Stage 3

At the start of Key Stage 3 the majority of pupils will have reached at least Level 4 in history. By the end of Key Stage 3 most pupils should be within the range of Levels 4–7.

- **Levels 5–6** are the target for 14-year-olds.
- **Level 8** is the standard reached by very able pupils.
- Exceptionally talented pupils can reach the **Exceptional Performance** category.

Use our checklist on the next page to assess the level you have reached by ticking the skills that you have mastered. It is written in easy-to-understand language.

Level	Change and Situations	Causes and Consequences	Interpretations of History	Uses of Evidence	Study Skills in History
4	I can talk, draw and write about the periods studied. I can describe events, people, changes and features.	I can provide several reasons for an event happening and I can describe its results.	I know different people can have different opinions about a past event and represent it differently.	I can select appropriate sources to find out about the past.	I am starting to plan my written work and I am using dates and historical terms.
5	I can describe and understand the past in more detail, and I am starting to show how changes and other aspects of the topics are linked.	I can show that some reasons or results of an event may be connected.	I can show that different people have different ideas about the past and that they have reasons for their opinions.	I can decide whether sources are useful or not for my purpose.	I can select the information which I think is important and organise it to produce a planned piece of work. I can use dates and historical terms.
6	I can use my knowledge to describe features and changes and I can show similarities and differences between periods and countries.	I can examine, consider and discuss the different reasons for and results of an event or change.	I can describe and explain the different ways in which people have viewed events, personalities and changes to societies or countries.	I can use my knowledge to decide whether a source is useful and use the source to increase my knowledge and reach conclusions.	I can select and make use of relevant information to produce well-organised work, using dates and historical terms.
7	I can link what I know in outline and use this knowledge to identify how differing features of the past are related. I can use this knowledge to investigate and comment on reasons and results.		I can describe different people's views about an event and explain clearly why they have different views.	I am starting to investigate questions on my own and I am using my own knowledge to select sources and information.	I can select and make use of relevant information to produce structured work which explains events. I can use dates and historical terms well.
8	I can use my outline and detailed knowledge to analyse links between events, people and changes. I can explain reasons for and results of changes and events.		I can explain why different people interpret an event differently. I can draw my own conclusions on which interpretation is best.	I can confidently investigate historical problems on my own. By using knowledge and judgement I can select the most useful and reliable evidence. I can draw my own conclusions.	I can select and make use of relevant information to produce consistently well-structured narrative, description and explanation. I can use a wide range of historical terms and key dates.

Exceptional Performance

I can use my extensive and detailed knowledge and understanding to analyse relationships between a wide range of events, people, ideas, changes and features in past societies. I can use a wide range of evidence to back up explanations of reasons and results. I can analyse links between events and developments in different countries and different periods.

I can make balanced judgements about the value of different interpretations of the past, and relate them to the historical context. I can make independent enquiries using sources to reach balanced and substantiated conclusions. I can select, organise and use a wide range of relevant information to produce consistently well-structured work, with good use of dates and terms.

Index

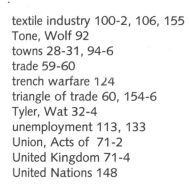

Acknowledgements

The author and publisher are grateful to the copyright holders, as credited, for permission to use quoted materials and photographs.

BBC: 6.6, 6.10

Mary Evans Picture Library: 1.2, 1.3, 1.4, 1.8, 1.11, 1.12, 1.14, 1.17, 1.18, 1.19, 1.21, 1.24, 1.25, 1.27, 1.30, 1.32, 1.34, 1.36, 1.39, 2.2, 2.3, 2.5, 2.11, 2.15, 2.17, 2.18, 2.19, 2.21, 2.22, 2.24, 2.26, 2.31, 3.2, 3.3, 3.5, 3.8, 4.10, 4.11, 4.8, 4.9, 4.14, 4.15, 4.16, 4.19, 4.20, 4.21, 4.25, 4.26, 4.27, 5.1, 5.2, 5.11, 5.18, 6.2, 6.3, 6.11, 6.12

Imperial War Museum: 5.8, 5.12, 5.17, 5.20, 5.24, 5.19, 5.32, 5.33

specialist publishing services (photographic) ltd: 1.44, 2.14, 3.10, 1.26, 1.23, 4.6, 4.17, 4.22

© of the trustees of the Goodwood Collection at West Sussex Record Office: 4.4

Dedication

The author would like to dedicate this book to his father 'for showing me the way' and to students and colleagues at Parkstone Grammar School.